INSTANT MATH

For Beginning Skills And Concepts
Hands-On Manipulative Activities

by Sam Ed Brown

Incentive Publications, Inc.
Nashville, Tennessee

Illustrated by Marta Johnson
Cover by Susan Eaddy

ISBN 0-86530-206-5

© Copyright 1991 by Incentive Publications, Inc., Nashville, TN. All rights reserved. No part of this publication may be reproduced, stored in a retrieval system, or transmitted in any form or by any means (electronic, mechanical, photocopying, recording, or otherwise) without prior written permission from Incentive Publications, Inc., with the exception below.

Permission is hereby granted to the purchaser of one copy of INSTANT MATH FOR BEGINNING SKILLS AND CONCEPTS to reproduce in sufficient quantities to meet yearly classroom needs.

Table of Contents

Preface ix

CARDINAL NUMBERS
Personal Manipulative Holder 12
Big Foot 13
The Button Box 14
Stories And Numbers 15
The Clothespin Game 16
Counting And Eating Fruits And Veggies 17
Counting With Stories 18
How Does It Work? 19
Number Order 20
Counting Worms 21
Eggs And All 22
Number Hunting 23
Number Garden 24
Beans And Math 25
Number Sentences 26
More Color Counting 27
Color Collage 28
Peanut Bingo 29
Can You Match It? 30
Counting Sticks 31

GRAPHING AND CHARTING
Human Bar Graphs 34
What's Your Favorite Kind? 35
Brown Eyes/Blue Eyes 36
Simple Graphs 37
Reds, Yellows, Or Greens 38
How Did You Get Here? 39
Attraction? 40
Classification Using The Senses 41
Charting The Room 42
Graphing Legs 43
Making Number Charts 44
More Than Or Fewer Than 45

COUNTING
Numerals And Numbers 48
Counting Leaves 49
Nursery Rhyme Numbers 50
Listening, Counting, And Recording 51
Counting Fingers 52
The Little Engine That Could 53

ESTIMATION
- Estimation And Thinking Skills 56
- Patterns And Predictions 57
- Cans Of Sand 58
- Halloween Pumpkin Strips 59
- Estimating Gummy Bits 60
- Thumbs Up/Thumbs Down 61
- The Estimation Game 62
- Watching Things Grow 63

MEASUREMENT
- Measuring And Eating 66
- Spring Sprouts 67
- Measuring With "Feet" 68
- Big Measuring Day 69
- Whose Shirt Is This? 70
- Predicting And Comparing 71
- Bean Potpourri 72
- Cotton Swab Measuring 73
- Do Things Change Size? 74
- Wholes Plus A Part 75
- Toothpaste Stretch 76
- Let's Look And Compare 77

MONEY AND TIME
- Buried Treasure 80
- Chain Of Days 81
- Playing With Time 82
- How Much Is It? 83

ORDINAL NUMBERS
- "Ordering" A Hamburger 86
- Ordinal Sandwiches 87
- Ordering The Ordinals 88
- Ghosts And Ordinal Numbers 89
- Ordinal Balloons 90
- What Is Missing? 91

SETS
- Making And Recognizing Sets 94
- Two Of What? 95
- Making Patterns 96
- Combining Like Sets 97
- Making Sets 98
- My Leg Book 99
- Apple Trees 100
- Big Blues And Little Yellows 101

SHAPE AND SIZE
Wind Chimes 104
Feed The Shape Box 105
Freehand Decorated Shape Necklaces 106
Counting The Wind 107
Shapes 108
Time For Pilgrims Again 109
Finding Shapes 110
Making Patterns 111
Talking Shapes 112
Simple Shapes 113
Making Shapes And Eating 114
Shaping The Outside 115
Tossing On The Sheet 116
Math Mobiles 117

SIMPLE MATHEMATICAL OPERATIONS USING MANIPULATIVES
Grab, Guess, And Count 120
Counting The Pins 121
Counting And Recording 122
Necklace Or Bracelet 123
Making A Counting Apparatus 124
My Name Is Two 125
Bean Race 126
Using The Number Line 127
Simple Sentence Problems - Subtraction 128
Mathematical Train 129
Starting In The Middle 130
Playing With Toothpicks 131

MISCELLANEOUS
Eat And Create 134
Where Is It? 135
Representational Math 136
Positional Simon Says 137
A Part Of A Whole 138
Flannel Board Positional 139
Beans And Peas 140
Building Fences 141

Bibliography 142

PREFACE

Many kindergarten and first and second grade teachers react with surprise when children who have learned to count and do very well solving problems using manipulatives, seem to have a great deal of difficulty with simple written problems in addition and subtraction.

Some children can solve the written problems, even with difficulty, and some children act as if the written problems are beyond them.

This is not a new phenomena in our schools. This problem is one that has always been present and is a contributor to what we sometimes call "mathphobia."

This book attempts some explanation for the problems teachers face and also, hopefully, offers solutions as well. It is not a "new math," but rather a relook, if you will, at what we know about young children, how they learn, and some things we should be doing in the mathematics area.

CARDINAL NUMBERS

- Personal Manipulative Holder ...12
- Big Foot 13
- The Button Box 14
- Stories And Numbers............15
- The Clothespin Game 16
- Counting And Eating Fruits And Veggies.....................17
- Counting With Stories 18
- How Does It Work? 19
- Number Order 20
- Counting Worms 21
- Eggs And All..................22
- Number Hunting 23
- Number Garden 24
- Beans And Math................25
- Number Sentences 26
- More Color Counting 27
- Color Collage 28
- Peanut Bingo..................29
- Can You Match It?..............30
- Counting Sticks...............31

PERSONAL MANIPULATIVE HOLDER

WHAT YOU'RE TEACHING:

Constructing personal holder for manipulatives, small motor development, artistic creativity, problem-solving

MATERIALS NEEDED:

Two egg cartons per child, buttons, pasta wheel shapes, dry detergent, tempera paint, glue, styrofoam cups, felt-tip pens

WHAT YOU DO:

Instruct the children to decorate their manipulative holders (egg cartons) as they wish. If the egg cartons are plastic, add powdered detergent to tempera paint so the paint will stick to the plastic. Children may use anything to decorate their holders.
To make different colored round discs, use the pasta wheels and mix several colors of tempera paint in styrofoam cups. Let the pasta soak overnight.
The next day lay the pasta on newspapers to dry. Other shapes of pasta may be used, colored or not, for counters. Let children bring buttons from home to use for counters. Allow the children to use their imagination for collecting items to use.
Store different types of counters in the decorated manipulative holders (egg cartons). Use the manipulative holders for math activities.

WHAT TO TALK ABOUT:

How manipulatives can help you learn.

BIG FOOT

WHAT YOU'RE TEACHING:

To reinforce counting, measurement skills, size concepts, metric measure practice

MATERIALS NEEDED:

A book about dinosaurs, butcher paper, yardstick, meterstick, felt-tip pens, black crayons, different colored construction paper, tape, toothpicks, and tongue depressors

WHAT YOU DO:

Read one or more fact books about dinosaurs. Talk about dinosaur tracks and how big they are (this should be found in the book).
Let the children make dinosaur tracks. Spread butcher paper on the floor. Use a picture from the book, a yardstick, and a meterstick to help the children draw an outline of a dinosaur track. Compare the measurement using a yardstick and a meterstick. Allow the children to color the track(s) black with crayon. Next, pass out the construction paper and have the children take off their shoes and socks and trace one of their feet on construction paper. Then let the children cut out their footprints and put their names on them. Put the dinosaur track on the wall and the children's footprints in the dinosaur tracks. Compare the sizes.

WHAT TO TALK ABOUT:

Discuss the size of the dinosaur track and the size of the human foot. Talk about the differences in measuring with a yardstick and a meterstick.

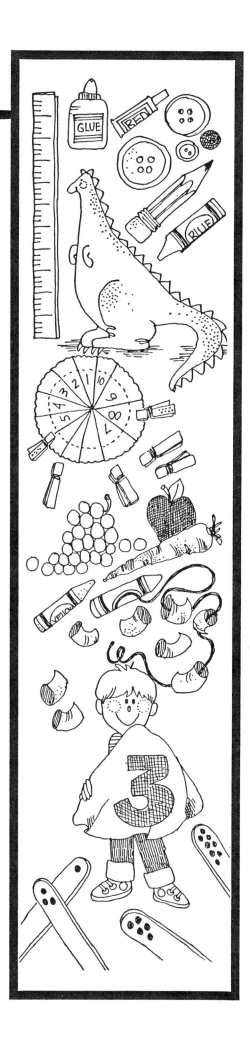

THE BUTTON BOX

WHAT YOU'RE TEACHING:

Counting, classification, vocabulary development

MATERIALS NEEDED:

Lots of buttons

WHAT YOU DO:

Divide the children into small groups and give each group a bunch of buttons. Instruct the children to group the buttons according to size, color, number of holes, and any other classifications they can think of. Encourage the children to discuss ways to classify the buttons. To extend the activity, help the children construct a bar graph using the buttons.

WHAT TO TALK ABOUT:

Different ways the children choose to classify their bunch of buttons. Can anyone think of another way?

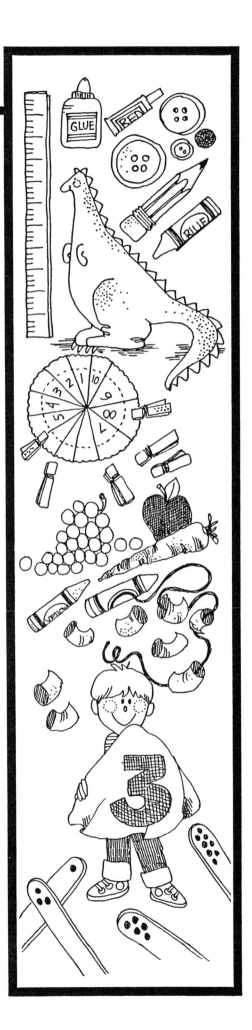

STORIES AND NUMBERS

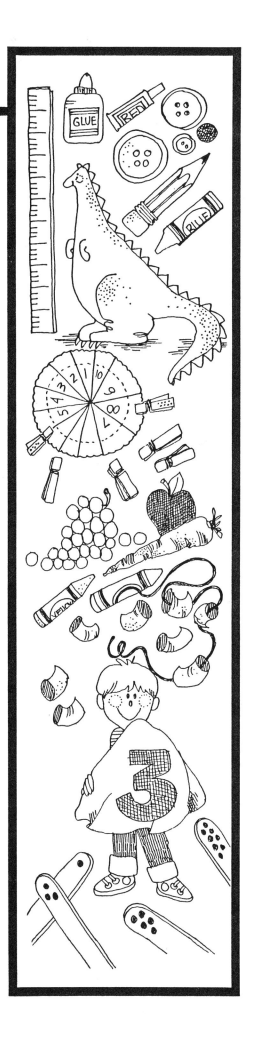

WHAT YOU'RE TEACHING:

Number concepts, creative thinking, creative writing, figure discrimination

MATERIALS NEEDED:

Various pictures (Some pictures should have more than one of the same item and some should have only one item of a kind.)

WHAT YOU DO:

Show a few of the pictures and talk with the children about the pictures. After showing a few of the pictures, let the children play a sentence game. Tell them you will hold up a picture, point out and name one item in the picture, and then call one volunteer to make up a complete sentence about that item.

After showing a few pictures and getting responses from the children, tell them you will now try and fool them. Tell them that when you point to and name an item that there just might be another item like it in the picture. If the children see two or three of the same items in the same picture, then they should not be fooled but make up as many sentences about the picture as there are different items.

Give the children two or three examples where they could be fooled, then begin calling on them. To extend the activity, supply paper for writing and construction paper for book covers. Encourage the children to select a picture they like and to draw it or write a story about it. Or let the children make up a story if they would rather.

WHAT TO TALK ABOUT:

How pictures can tell stories. Discuss number concepts - one's, two's, etc.

THE CLOTHESPIN GAME

WHAT YOU'RE TEACHING:

Number recognition, number concepts, matching, and learning word names

MATERIALS NEEDED:

Paper plates, ruler, felt-tip pens, clothespins

WHAT TO DO:

Divide several paper plates into ten sections; put a number word on each section beginning with one. Match each number word with an equal number of dots made with a felt-tip pen. On each clothespin, match the numeral with an equal number of dots. Encourage the children to match and clip the clothespins with the correct match on the paper plate. Children should check each other's work.

WHAT TO TALK ABOUT:

How numerals name numbers, how groups of objects can be named with a number word.

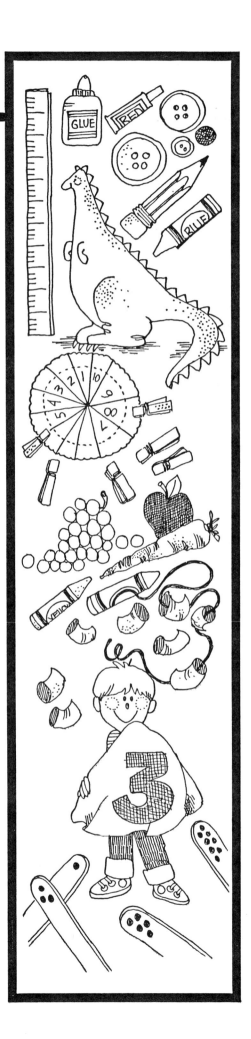

COUNTING AND EATING FRUITS AND VEGGIES

WHAT YOU'RE TEACHING:

Counting, classification, sorting

MATERIALS NEEDED:

Carrots, bell peppers, celery, apples, grapes, and other fruits and vegetables; old magazines and catalogs; glue; scissors; construction paper; plastic serrated knives; plastic sandwich bags

WHAT YOU DO:

Brainstorm different fruits and vegetables with the children, and list their answers on an experience chart. Let the children bring one or two vegetables or fruits to school. The day before, have catalogs, magazines, and newspapers available for the children to cut out pictures of fruits and vegetables and glue them to construction paper. Help them draw lines on the back of the pictures, number the pieces, and cut them out to make puzzle pieces. Place each puzzle in its own plastic sandwich bag. Let the children put their puzzles together and swap with others so they can work several puzzles.
The next day when the children bring in their fruits and vegetables, put them on a table, and let everyone match the puzzles with the real fruits and vegetables by giving the children serrated knives and helping them cut the matched fruits and vegetables into similar puzzles. Store these in plastic sandwich bags, and allow the children to put together the actual food puzzles, also. To extend the activity, provide water and small brushes for the children to clean the fruits and vegetables. Then let them put together a puzzle and eat it and/or cut the fruits and vegetables into small pieces and make a fruit and vegetable salad.

WHAT TO TALK ABOUT:

How vegetables and fruit can help us learn counting.

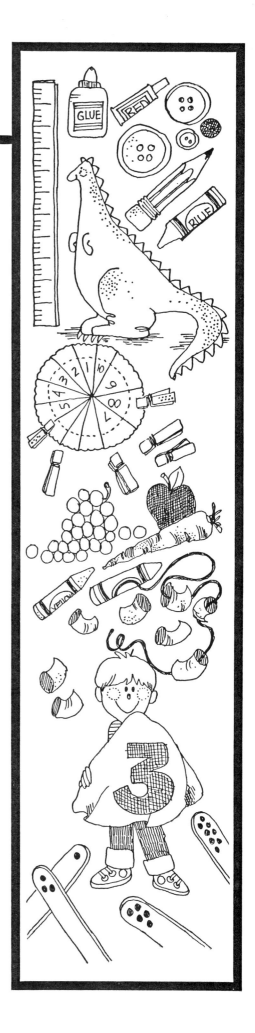

COUNTING WITH STORIES

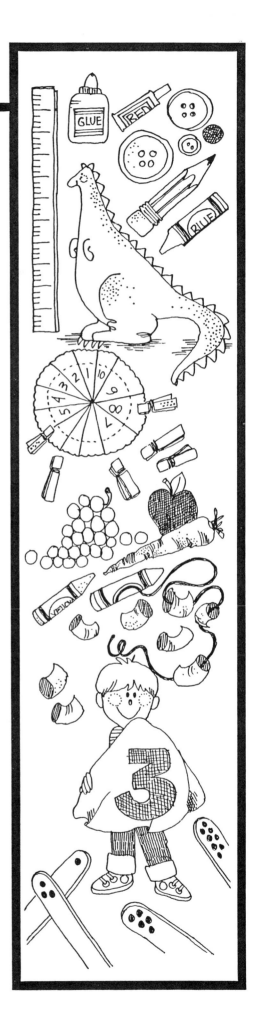

WHAT YOU'RE TEACHING:

One-to-one correspondence, counting, number concepts, auditory memory

MATERIALS NEEDED:

Children's books related to counting and manipulation such as *The Three Bears, Three Little Pigs, Caps For Sale,* etc; flannel board, flannel cutouts for each story used

WHAT YOU DO:

Read the children a story. Tell them you need help telling the story with the flannel board.
Put up your flannel board and lay all of the pieces for the story on a table. Tell the children you will start to tell the story and will call on volunteers to help you put up the correct pictures.
Start reading the story, and when you come to a place where a flannel cutout should be used, pause and ask who knows what should be placed on the board, e.g., the three bear's chairs, then let a volunteer count and put up the pieces. Continue with the same story or another story so every child has a chance to participate. To extend the activity, give the children felt, cardboard, and glue. Help them make their own flannel boards. Show them how, and help them cut out pictures (handdrawn or cut out of magazines), and glue felt on the back to make a flannel board cutout.
Children can retell stories, or they can use the handdrawn pictures and make up stories of their own. Let them share their creations with the rest of the class.

WHAT TO TALK ABOUT:

Talk about the flannel pieces used with the stories.

HOW DOES IT WORK?

WHAT YOU'RE TEACHING:

Exploring math processes, counting with concrete objects, learning number concepts

MATERIALS NEEDED:

Large and medium-sized uncooked macaroni, string, crayons, glue, scissors

WHAT YOU DO:

Show the children how to make necklaces and bracelets. (Let them first cut lengths of string for the necklaces and bracelets and tell them to dip one end of the string into the glue and let it dry. This will make the string stiff on the end and easier to handle.)
Children should use crayons to color their macaroni. Then let them "string" their macaroni. Each necklace and bracelet should have a number name, such as a "seven bracelet" or a "twelve necklace." (Base this on the number of macaroni pieces used to make each item.) To extend the activity, use other items in addition to macaroni, such as small shapes (circles, triangles, squares, rectangles), popcorn, raisins, etc. Shapes offer a new concept combined with the counting and number process.
Popcorn can be popped in the classroom which adds science and cooking to the activity.

WHAT TO TALK ABOUT:

The process used to make jewelry, how/why could counting be an important part of jewelry making.

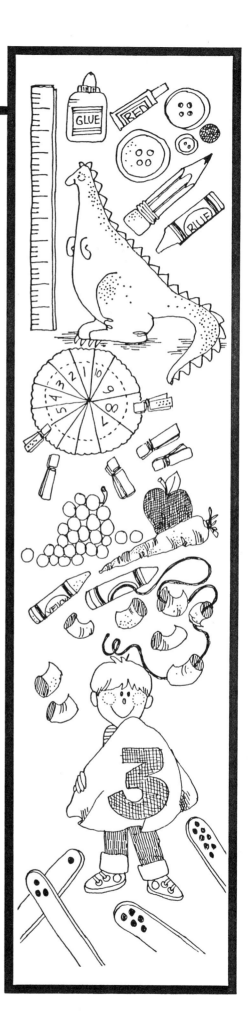

NUMBER ORDER

WHAT YOU'RE TEACHING:

Number recognition, sequential order, number names, counting

MATERIALS NEEDED:

Old magazines, newspapers, catalogs, index cards, glue, scissors

WHAT YOU DO:

Let the children cut numbers from magazines, catalogs, and newspapers. Have them glue each number they find to an index card. Let the children work in groups to lay the numbers face-up.
Then let them take turns sequencing the numbers as far as they can count. The children soon will be able to do this by themselves. To extend the activity, have a number day where all the activities deal with numbers: number cooking - cookies shaped like numbers; number art - make all art projects using numbers and shapes; social studies - discuss general numbers such as speed limits, phone numbers, addresses; language arts - point out numbers found in story books.

WHAT TO TALK ABOUT:

Sequencing, number order

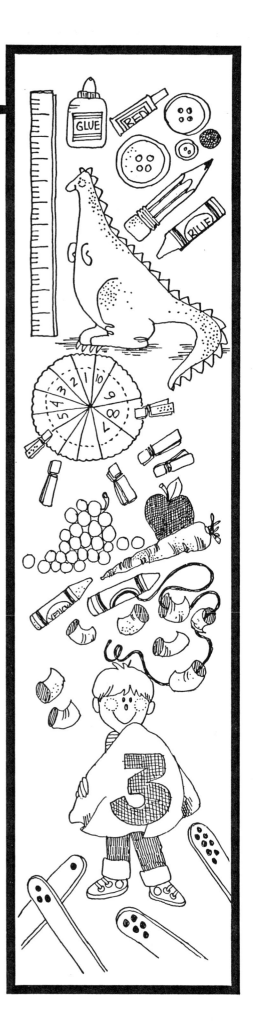

COUNTING WORMS

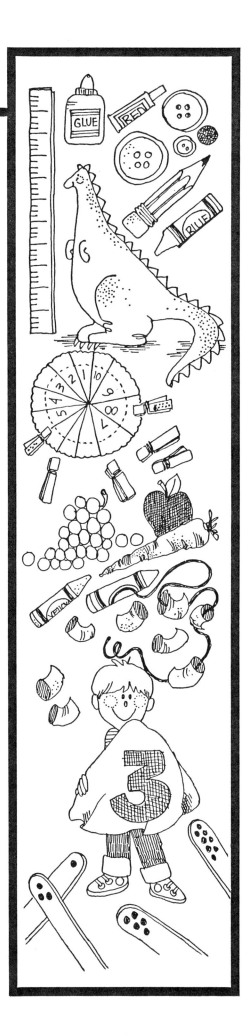

WHAT YOU'RE TEACHING:

Counting, sorting

MATERIALS NEEDED:

Several packages of gummy worms, ten styrofoam cups, felt-tip pens

WHAT YOU DO:

Line the cups on the chalk ledge after numbering them from one to ten. On a table next to the cups, pile the gummy worms together. Let each child come forward and count out the correct number of gummy worms to put in the specific cup you have chosen. If the child does this correctly, let him eat a gummy worm.

WHAT TO TALK ABOUT:

How the worms feel. Do real worms feel different? Real worms don't live in a sack; where do they live? Would a real worm taste like a gummy worm?

EGGS AND ALL

WHAT YOU'RE TEACHING:

Counting, matching numerals and objects, and matching numerals

MATERIALS NEEDED:

Egg carton, large plastic egg, twelve small plastic eggs, beans, felt-tip pen

WHAT YOU DO:

Number the egg cups inside the egg carton from left to right beginning with the inside row and finishing with the outside row. Fill the large plastic egg with beans. Number the small plastic eggs from one to twelve.
Let the children put the same number of beans into the appropriate numbered small egg and then place that egg into the matching egg cup in the egg carton. This teaches the children to match numbers and objects. Let the children check each other's work.

WHAT TO TALK ABOUT:

Discuss how many is in a dozen. What do your parents buy at the store by the dozen? (Eggs, oranges.) Does a dozen eggs contain the same number as a dozen oranges?

NUMBER HUNTING

WHAT YOU'RE TEACHING:

Number recognition, making sets

MATERIALS NEEDED:

Large numbers cut from different colored poster board, felt, terry cloth or old sheeting, permanent marker, scissors, clothespins

WHAT YOU DO:

Cut out 3' x 2' capes for the children. Hold capes together with clothespins. Help the children write a number from one to ten on the back of their capes. The children should try to guess the number on their capes by clues from other children.
Have the children line up in sequence and arrange themselves into like sets. There should be mostly sets of two's and some three's.
While the children close their eyes, "hide" large numeral cutouts. Allow the children to search until they find the same numeral they have on the back of their capes.

WHAT TO TALK ABOUT:

Talk about numerals, ordering from one to ten, like sets.

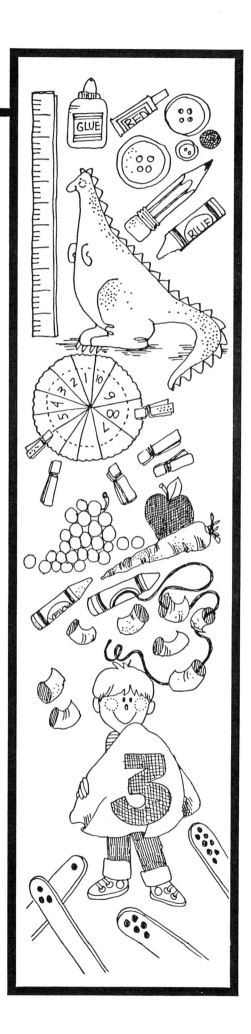

NUMBER GARDEN

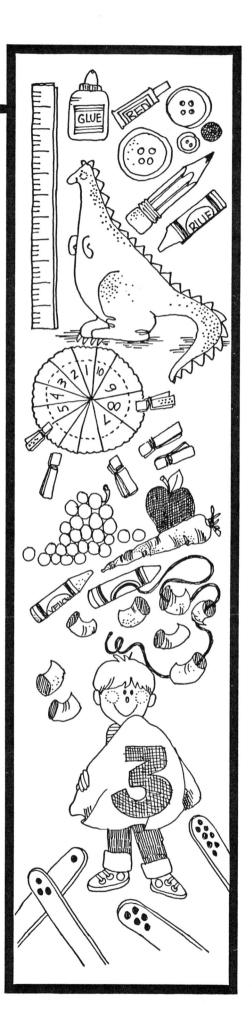

WHAT YOU'RE TEACHING:

Counting, numeral recognition, left/right brain integration

MATERIALS NEEDED:

Cardboard boxes (2 inches high), shallow TV dinner trays, potting soil, sand, grass seed

WHAT YOU DO:

This activity allows the children to plant and grow their own number(s) of choice. Give each child a container of his own. Explain that everybody will grow their own number.
Mix potting soil with sand for a growing medium. Put about an inch of the mixture into each child's container. Show the children how they can use their finger to draw at least two numerals in their soil. Put out bowls of grass seed and allow the children to spread a line of seed in the numbers they made with their fingers. Next, have the children cover the seeds with soil and water their number garden. If cardboard containers are used, they can be lined with plastic.
Put the gardens in well-lighted areas, and within a few days the children should see their number gardens grow!

WHAT TO TALK ABOUT:

Planting, numbers "feeling" numbers. What is necessary for plants to grow?

BEANS AND MATH

WHAT YOU'RE TEACHING:

Simple addition, joining sets, counting for a total

MATERIALS NEEDED:

Thirty dried beans for each child, small paper cups, yarn

WHAT YOU DO:

Give each child three paper cups, and instruct each to place a piece of yarn around the three cups. Tell the children to put ten beans in each cup. Then ask the children to pour out the beans in their three cups into one pile and count them.

WHAT TO TALK ABOUT:

How three sets of ten beans turned into thirty beans. What would happen if fewer beans were in each cup? If more beans were in each cup?

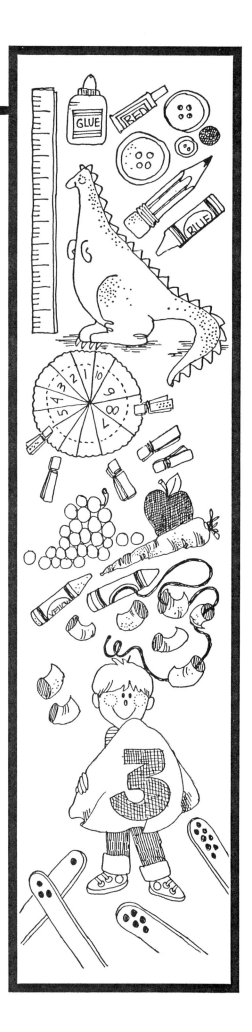

NUMBER SENTENCES

WHAT YOU'RE TEACHING:

Counting, auditory and visual memory, writing skills

MATERIALS NEEDED:

Ten pieces of white construction paper numbered from one to ten with a marker, a package of plain construction paper, regular white paper, pencils, stapler, crayons

WHAT YOU DO:

Tell the children to help you make number sentences. Hold up the paper with the number "4" and say, "I saw four cats on the way to school this morning," as an example. Continue giving examples until the children understand what to do.
When the children are ready, choose individuals, show them a number, and ask them to say their number sentences aloud to the class. Encourage the children to make up stories about their number.
Fold a piece of construction paper and two pieces of plain white paper together, staple, and make each child a book. Allow the children to write and/or draw their stories in individual books.

WHAT TO TALK ABOUT:

Making sentences and books with numbers.

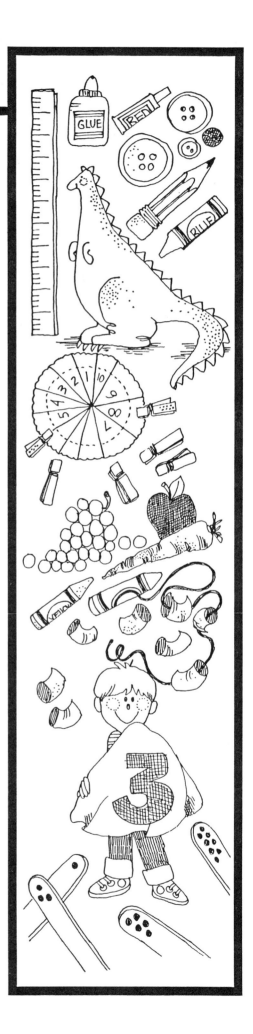

MORE COLOR COUNTING

WHAT YOU'RE TEACHING:

Relating a child's natural interest in color to counting

MATERIALS NEEDED:

A 4" x 12" x 2" block of wood, six 1/2" dowels (8 inches in length), wood curtain rings, glue, drill, paintbrushes, and paint for each primary color. Drill six holes for dowels in the block of wood before beginning the activity.

WHAT YOU DO:

Allow the children to make the "color counter." Explain to them how you make the holes in the wooden block. Show them how they fit. Put out the dowels, wooden rings, and paint. Help the children paint each of the dowels a different color. Next, help them paint at least ten wooden rings for each colored dowel.

Beginning the next day, start a color survey. Say to the group, "Who has on something red today?" Each child with red on should come forward and place a red ring on the red dowel. Do this with each color until all the children have participated. Next, allow different children to count the rings on each dowel. Record the number they count. After all the dowels have been counted and recorded, say, "We have six rings on the red, four on the blue, etc."

Next say, "I wonder how many there are on all the color sticks?" Write the number on the board in the form of a problem, and then help the children count all the rings. Record the answer. Allow children to do this activity when they have time during the day.

WHAT TO TALK ABOUT:

Discuss what colors the children like best. Talk about how a dowel forms a set of a certain color. Talk about classification – the children putting colors on different dowels is a form of classifying.

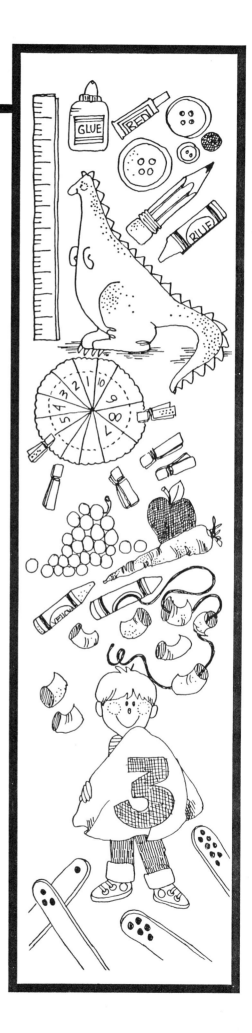

COLOR COLLAGE

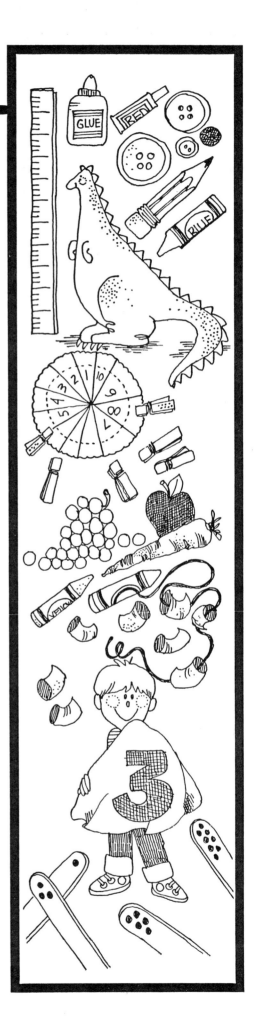

WHAT YOU'RE TEACHING:

Classification, reinforcing color concepts, counting

MATERIALS NEEDED:

Old magazines, scissors, glue, brown construction paper, picture of colored leaves

WHAT YOU DO:

Discuss the fall season with the children. Ask them what colors they see on plants in the fall. Show them the picture of the colored leaves on the trees. Allow the children to cut pictures from the magazines that remind them of fall colors. Let the children glue their pictures on brown construction paper. Have them write their names and the number of items they cut out under their pictures.

WHAT TO TALK ABOUT:

Why do leaves change color? When do leaves change color? What are other signs of fall? Which season follows fall? Which season comes before fall?

PEANUT BINGO

WHAT YOU'RE TEACHING:

Counting, number recognition, letter recognition, gamesmanship

MATERIALS NEEDED:

Dry roasted peanuts, construction paper, ink pen

WHAT YOU DO:

Work together to make the cards for the game. Large Bingo cards with randomly placed numbers should be used in the beginning. The teacher or a student can use a deck of cards with the face cards removed to call numbers at random. Groups of five or six should play at a time. As the students hear a number called on their card, they should use a peanut to put on that number. Use regular Bingo rules. Let the children eat their peanuts at the end of the game. Later, after the children become skilled at using numbers, use letters. A variety of five letter words may be substituted for the word Bingo, e.g., "table."

WHAT TO TALK ABOUT:

Identifying numbers, playing by the rules, sing the song "Bingo," substitute other words for the word Bingo, talk about numerals when used in a game like Bingo.

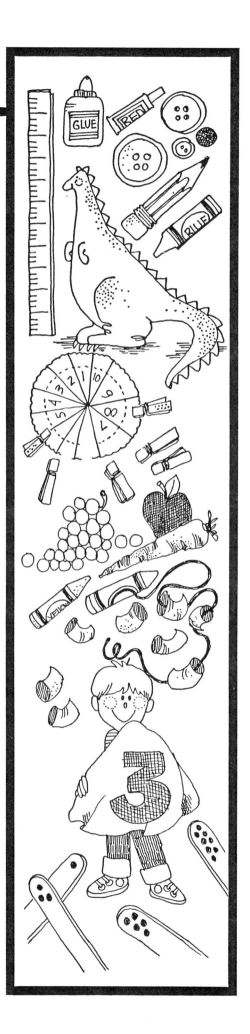

CAN YOU MATCH IT?

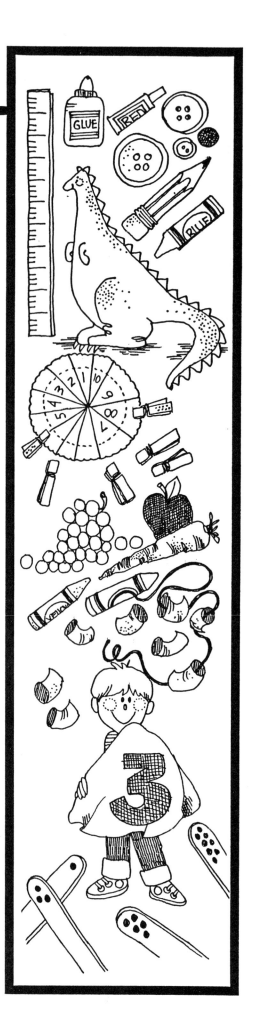

WHAT YOU'RE TEACHING:

Counting, number recognition, number concepts

MATERIALS NEEDED:

Construction paper; stickers of various kinds like stars, flags, or other concrete objects; felt-tip pen

WHAT YOU DO:

Number ten sheets of construction paper from one to ten. Put stickers on about forty pieces of construction paper. Each sheet should have one to ten stickers. Select one child to be "It," and give that child the construction paper sheets with the numbers one through ten. Seat the rest of the children in a semicircle in front of "It." Pass out the sheets with the stickers. The object of the game is for "It" to match any card with objects with a number card. Children take turns holding up a card with a number of stickers, and "It" must hold up the matching number card that matches the number of stickers on the paper. If "It" misses, the child holding the concept card becomes "It." If no one misses after everyone has had a turn, "It" gets to select someone to take his place.

WHAT TO TALK ABOUT:

Discuss the relationship between numbers and objects. Discuss what numbers can name.

COUNTING STICKS

WHAT YOU'RE TEACHING:

Counting, one-to-one correspondence, number recognition

MATERIALS NEEDED:

Ten cups, fifty-five tongue depressors, felt-tip pen

WHAT YOU DO:

Using a felt-tip pen, make one dot on one stick, two dots on two sticks, three dots on three sticks, etc., until you have put ten dots on ten sticks. Number the cups one through ten. Let different groups of children count the dots on the sticks and put the stick in the cup numbered correspondingly.

WHAT TO TALK ABOUT:

Talk about number concepts. Are four blocks the same number as four tongue depressors?

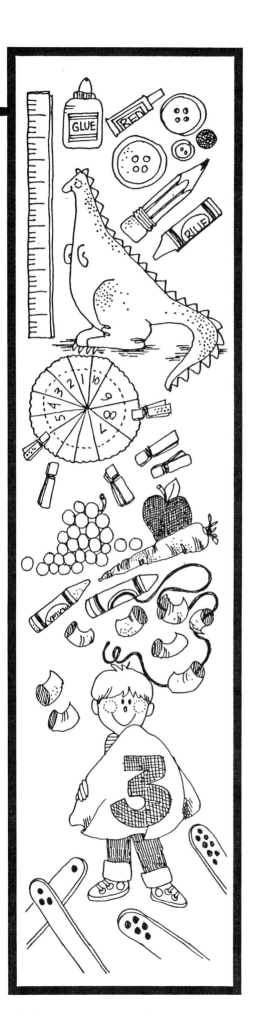

GRAPHING AND CHARTING

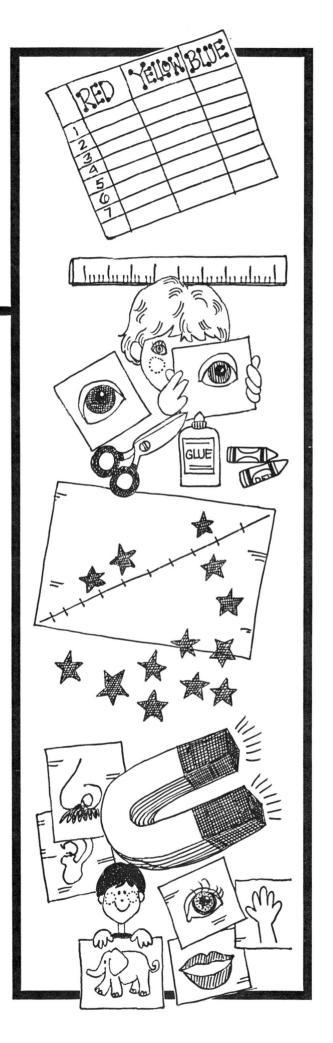

- Human Bar Graphs 34
- What's Your Favorite Kind? 35
- Brown Eyes/Blue Eyes 36
- Simple Graphs 37
- Reds, Yellows, Or Greens 38
- How Did You Get Here? 39
- Attraction? 40
- Classification Using
  The Senses 41
- Charting The Room 42
- Graphing Legs 43
- Making Number Charts 44
- More Than Or Fewer Than 45

HUMAN BAR GRAPHS

WHAT YOU'RE TEACHING:

Bar graphs, counting

MATERIALS NEEDED:

Large piece of cardboard

WHAT YOU DO:

Introduce or reinforce bar graphs. Write at the top of the poster board the words: RED, YELLOW, BLUE, GREEN, BLACK, and BROWN. Divide the poster board into columns for each color. Number up the left-hand side from one to twenty-two beginning at the bottom. Help the children count the number of children who are wearing colors written on the poster. Then construct a bar graph.
Next, tell the children they will use themselves to make a human bar graph. Ask a simple question such as, "Would you like to have ice cream, chocolate cake, or candy?" Line up the children according to their answers. Let them look around and see that the three lines they made are a human bar graph.

WHAT TO TALK ABOUT:

Why we use bar graphs. What bar graphs tell us.

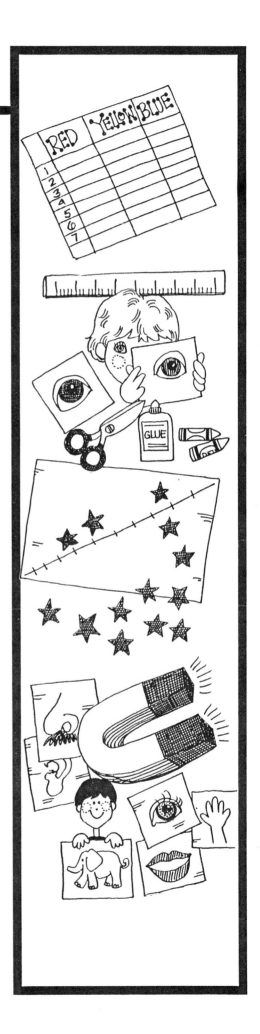

WHAT'S YOUR FAVORITE KIND?

WHAT YOU'RE TEACHING:

Graphing skills, counting, visual acuity

MATERIALS NEEDED:

Large piece of poster board, pictures of several different kinds of cars (at least six), felt-tip pens, paper, pencils

WHAT YOU DO:

Display the pictures of the cars you have brought in. Name and talk about each car. Draw six vertical lines on the poster board to divide it into six columns. Glue a picture of a car at the top of each column and print the name of the car underneath each picture. Pass out pieces of paper. Tell the children they will play a special game of counting cars. Tell them you want each to choose one car as their "special" car. After the children have made their choices, help them write the name of the car on their piece of paper. Try to see that there is almost equal representation for each car.

Explain to the children that at recess they will count cars that go by their school. Tell them to watch for the car on their papers, and every time they see one go by, they should put a mark on their paper.

Let them watch cars for about 10 minutes.

When the children return to the classroom, put the name of each car on the board, and take their papers and count the marks.

After counting, number the left side of the poster board from the bottom up (wait to number to be sure you know how many you will need or if you will number in single digits, two's, or five's, it will depend on the traffic). Next, let the children help you color in the number of cars seen in each column.

WHAT TO TALK ABOUT:

Graphing and the way it helps us use our eyes to see the answers to problems.

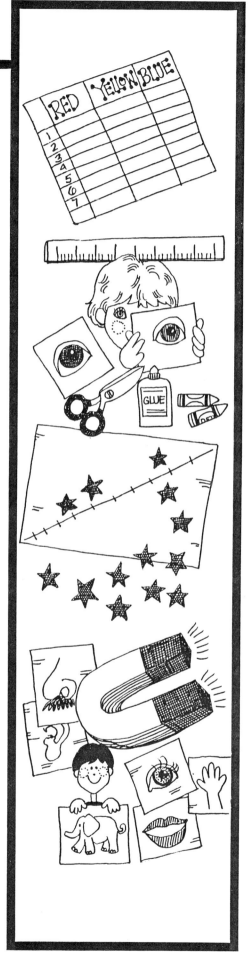

BROWN EYES/BLUE EYES

WHAT YOU'RE TEACHING:

Graphing, classifying, using math vocabulary, reinforcing color recognition

MATERIALS NEEDED:

Eye patterns for the children to color, crayons, large piece of poster board, construction paper, scissors, glue

WHAT YOU DO:

Have the children sort themselves according to eye color (some children do not know the color of their eyes). Pass out eye patterns and let the children draw their eyes and color them the appropriate color.
Make as many different vertical columns as there are different eye colors on the poster board. Glue an appropriate colored eye at the bottom of each column and the name of the color. Have the children "glue their eyes" in the correct column. Make graphs of their activities.

WHAT TO TALK ABOUT:

Talk about what a graph is (a picture of amounts). Read graphs, compare amounts, discuss "most" and "least."
Discuss families - talk about parents' eye color and brothers and sisters, etc.

SIMPLE GRAPHS

WHAT YOU'RE TEACHING:

Simple graphs, counting, simple measurement

MATERIALS NEEDED:

Package of construction paper 8-1/2" x 11" with two inches trimmed off the bottom; rulers with the inch marks marked with red ink; pencils; stars or other gummed markers

WHAT YOU DO:

Pass out a piece of construction paper with a dot in the upper left corner and a dot in the lower right corner and a ruler to each child. Tell the children they will draw a diagonal line from the upper left corner of their papers to the lower right corner. Have them lay their rulers across their paper from the upper left-hand corner to the lower right-hand corner and draw a line. (Demonstrate by holding a piece of construction paper flat against the chalkboard. Place your ruler correctly and draw a line.)

Next, tell the children to put a mark beside each red mark on the ruler; tell them this in an inch. Help them number the dots from one to ten along their lines. Pass out gummed markers, and help the children put the correct number of gummed markers to correspond to the numbers they have written. Then children should put them side-by-side beginning at the left side of the paper in a line beside the number.

WHAT TO TALK ABOUT:

How rulers should be used for measuring or drawing, diagonal means from corner to corner, why we usually draw from the left to the right.

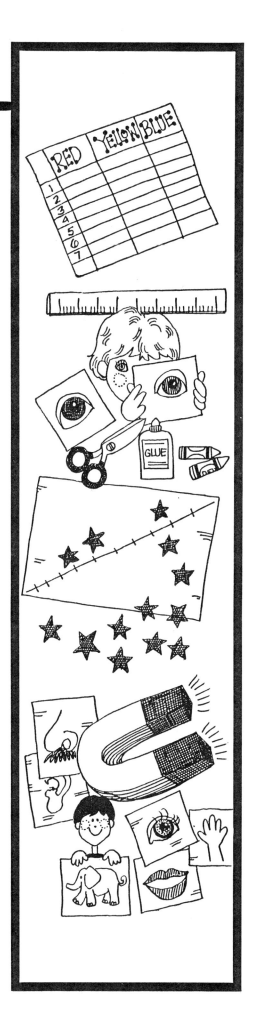

REDS, YELLOWS, OR GREENS

WHAT YOU'RE TEACHING:

Graphing, counting, visual memory

MATERIALS NEEDED:

A small piece of poster board, different colored felt-tip pens, watch

WHAT YOU DO:

Divide your children into three groups. Tell them that they will have a color race. Assign one color (red, yellow, or green) to each group. At recess, take the children out and tell them to count the number of children wearing the color assigned to their group. (Give them one minute to do this.) Tell them when to start and stop. Inside, have the groups sit together, and you help each group add the individual counts to get a group total.
Divide your poster board into three lengthwise sections. Put a color (red, yellow, green) at the top of each section. Number on the right of the chart. Ask each group the total number of children they saw wearing the color assigned to their group. Using colored felt-tip pens, color in the number counted by each group in the appropriate column to form a bar graph.

WHAT TO TALK ABOUT:

How you can use a bar graph to see the number counted. How you can tell which group counted the most and the least at a glance.

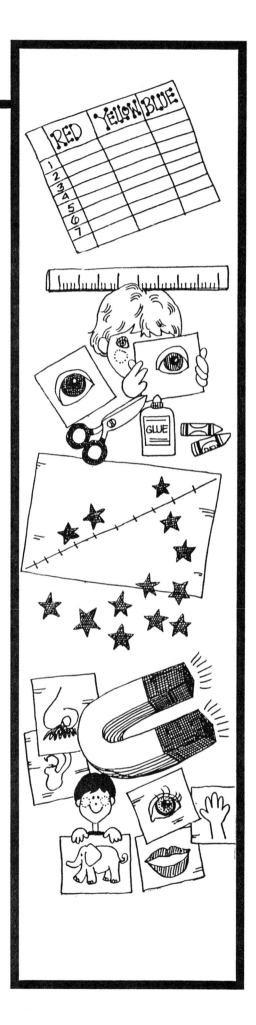

HOW DID YOU GET HERE?

WHAT YOU'RE TEACHING:

Graphing skills, counting, comparing, creative writing

MATERIALS NEEDED:

Large piece of poster board; pictures of a child walking, a car, a school bus; construction paper; plain paper; pencils; crayons; reusable adhesive

WHAT YOU DO:

This activity should increase skills as children notice different modes of transportation and how their classmates get to school. Divide the poster board into three columns, and head the columns with a picture of a child walking, a car, and a school bus. As the children come to school, instruct them to go over to a table in front of the chart, pick up their laminated name tags, and put their name tags under the corresponding column of transportation they used to get to school. (Children should notice how many students are not there.) To extend the activity, help the children make books by folding blank paper inside a folded piece of colored construction paper and stapling it together. Tell the children to write and/or draw a picture of something they saw on the way to school they had not noticed before.

WHAT TO TALK ABOUT:

How many more car riders are there than bus riders? Which group has more? Less? Are any groups the same? Discuss how carpooling or walking to school can help the environment.

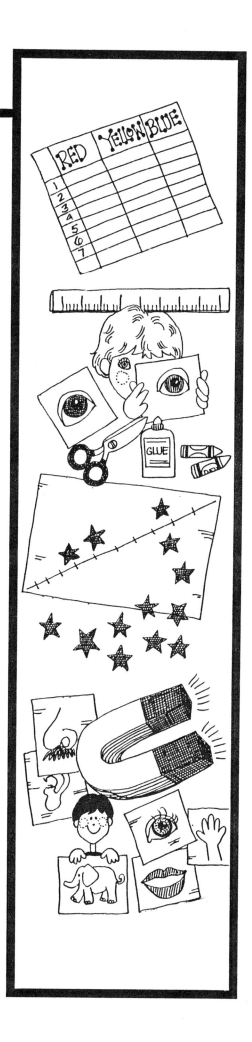

ATTRACTION?

WHAT YOU'RE TEACHING:

Classification, predicting, charting

MATERIALS NEEDED:

Magnet, assortment of small items that can and cannot be attracted by magnets, a large piece of cardboard, felt-tip markers

WHAT YOU DO:

Draw one vertical line from top to bottom on the cardboard and draw several horizontal lines across the board. Label one side of the cardboard "ATTRACTS" and the other side "DOES NOT ATTRACT." Put all the objects together, select one, and allow the children to find out if the magnet attracts that object. According to the results, lay the object on the proper place on the graph. Continue until all the items have been tested and are in the right place.

WHAT TO TALK ABOUT:

Magnetism, materials items are made from, graphing by placing objects in their proper places, and classifying by dividing objects into two groups.

CLASSIFICATION USING THE SENSES

WHAT YOU'RE TEACHING:

Classification, use of senses, charting

MATERIALS NEEDED:

Large piece of poster board, five small pieces of paper (4" x 4"), scissors, glue, marker, old magazines

WHAT YOU DO:

On each piece of paper, draw a part of the body that represents one of the five senses (nose, eye, ear, mouth, hand). On the poster board draw five vertical lines, and glue on one of the senses pictures at the top of each column. Encourage the children to look through the magazines and find pictures that relate to each sense. Have the children glue the picture in the appropriate place for classification and to create a senses chart.

WHAT TO TALK ABOUT:

Talk about the importance of classification and charting in mathematics. Have the children suggest ways we use classification and charting in math. Write the answers on the experience chart.

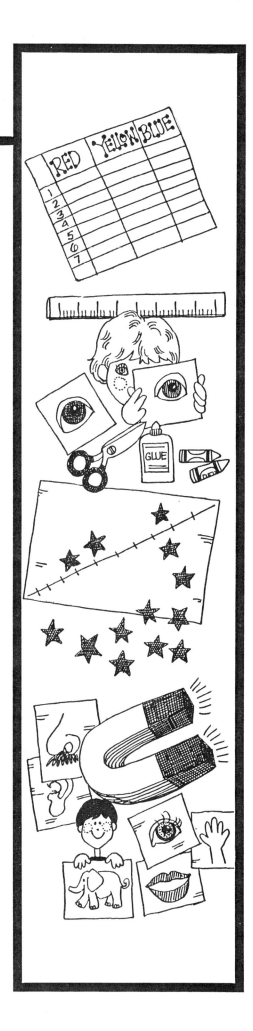

CHARTING THE ROOM

WHAT YOU'RE TEACHING:

Charting, measuring, observing, similarities and differences

MATERIALS NEEDED:

Tape measure, tagboard, markers

WHAT YOU DO:

Seat the children on the floor in front of an experience chart. Draw shapes the class has been studying (usually the circle, square, triangle, and rectangle). Talk to the children about other shapes. Encourage them to name other shapes, and if a child comes up with a divergent shape, allow him to draw and name that shape.
The children should choose one shape at a time to search for in the room and place its name on the chart. Let the children search for that particular shape in the room and place it on the tagboard chart when they find it.
After adding several shapes, the children should have a nice chart. If size restrictions are necessary, use a tape measure.

WHAT TO TALK ABOUT:

How shapes are alike and different — the same shape can be large or small. Shapes are everywhere, so we can make up names for shapes that do not already have names.

GRAPHING LEGS

WHAT YOU'RE TEACHING:

Counting, graphing, sorting/classification, deductive reasoning, math vocabulary

MATERIALS NEEDED:

Old magazines, picture books, catalogs, tape, scissors, large piece of poster board which has been divided by vertical lines into six columns

WHAT YOU DO:

Let the children find and cut out pictures of an animal, insect, or other living creature out of magazines. Have each child count the number of legs on his animal. Display the poster board which has been divided into six parts and numbered "0," "1," "2," "3," "4," "Many."
Let the children bring their pictures to the front of the room, name their animals, and tell how many legs it has. The child should then tape the picture in the appropriate column. To extend the activity, discuss animals in your science book. Read a book on animals for language arts. Discuss ways animals move as a social studies activity. Play records and act out animals and their "voices."

WHAT TO TALK ABOUT:

Discuss different animals, divide animals into groups, discuss bar graphs

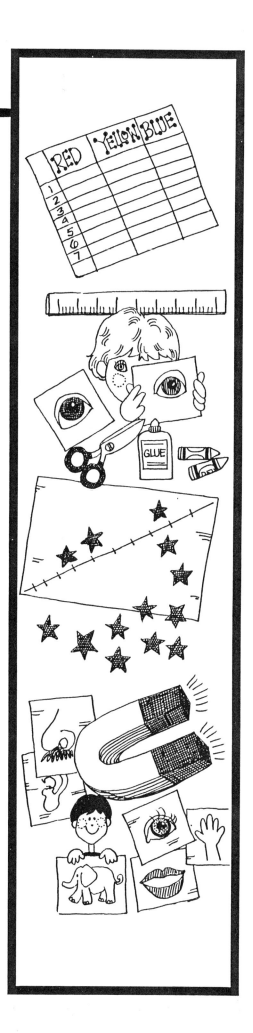

MAKING NUMBER CHARTS

WHAT YOU'RE TEACHING:

Counting practice, writing numbers practice, reinforcing left-to-right progression

MATERIALS NEEDED:

Sheets of chart paper divided horizontally into ten sections (enough for each child to have one with a few extras); crayons; pencils; glue; many small manipulatives such as beans, buttons, or other small objects

WHAT YOU DO:

Draw on the board a number chart like the ones the children will draw. Pass out the lined chart paper. Let the children number the sections from one to ten starting at the top.
Divide the children into groups and provide each group with many manipulatives. Ask the children to pick manipulatives of their choice and put the number of manipulatives beside the number. Help the children check the charts and their work. After all are correct, let the children glue the manipulatives to the chart. Place the charts in convenient places around the room for the children to use for reference. To extend the activity, read a number book to the children. Let them look through newspapers and cut out numbers. Let the children write recipes and try them out. Look for numbers in the environment (phone numbers, etc.)

WHAT TO TALK ABOUT:

How numbers tell us the number of items used. Numerals can be represented by using objects.

MORE THAN OR FEWER THAN

WHAT YOU'RE TEACHING:

More practice for charting, counting, math vocabulary (more than, fewer than)

MATERIALS NEEDED:

Poster board, plastic wrap, felt-tip pens, clothespins (spring-type), white paper, glue

WHAT YOU DO:

Use plastic wrap to cover a 4 inch strip across the top of the poster board. Divide this strip in half horizontally drawing a line with a felt-tip pen. Divide the poster board in half vertically with the pen. On the lower half of the divided plastic strip, print the word "Yes" on one half and "No" on the other half. Use the top half of the plastic wrap strip to write a statement that can be answered "Yes" or "No," such as, "My favorite food is cake." (Writing on the plastic strip enables you to wipe it clean to write another statement.)

Allow each child to write his name, cut it out, and glue it to a clothespin.

The teacher or child should read the statement to the children, and the children should respond to the statement by clipping their clothespins either to the "Yes" side or the "No" side of the poster board. Count the number of clothespins to see which has more and fewer. Record the answer. The children may brainstorm other yes/no questions or statements, wipe off the writing on the plastic wrap, and replace it with another challenge.

WHAT TO TALK ABOUT:

What "more than" and "less than" mean, charting. What does the word "majority" mean?

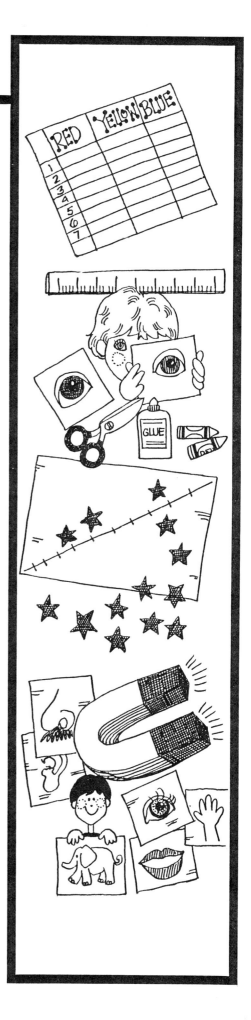

COUNTING

- Numerals And Numbers 48
- Counting Leaves 49
- Nursery Rhyme Numbers..........50
- Listening, Counting,
  And Recording 51
- Counting Fingers 52
- The Little Engine That Could 53

NUMERALS AND NUMBERS

WHAT YOU'RE TEACHING:

Understanding that numerals name numbers, using number concepts

MATERIALS NEEDED:

Large size construction paper numerals (1-9), rough sandpaper, large flat piece of styrofoam, 55 golf tees or pegs

WHAT YOU DO:

On each construction paper numeral, glue the corresponding number of dots cut from rough sandpaper. Explain the numerals and how each one names the number of sandpaper dots. Go through some "language patterns" with the children, such as "One, two, three, four, this is the numeral four.'" Explain that while the numeral "four" names the number of sandpaper dots the students can feel, it also names four of anything else. Challenge the children to take a numeral, count the sandpaper dots, and then find the same number of other things in the room such as blocks, pencils, toys, books, etc. Using a large sheet of styrofoam, make a number mat. With a permanent marker, write the numerals one through ten across the styrofoam. Mark under each numeral the corresponding number of dots. Put the mat with a box containing fifty-five golf tees or pegs where the children can use them during their free time. Demonstrate, and then let the children stick the corresponding number of pegs into the styrofoam.

WHAT TO TALK ABOUT:

Numerals name numbers.

COUNTING LEAVES

WHAT YOU'RE TEACHING:

Number recognition, one-to-one correspondence, counting, concepts about plants

MATERIALS NEEDED:

In advance, look at the young plants on a weeded lot. Try and find different plants with one to ten leaves on them.

WHAT YOU DO:

Put the plants on the windowsill in mixed order. Let the children take turns matching the number cards to the correct plant. Rearrange plants after each child matches. Have the children arrange the plants in ordinal arrangement. Identify as many plants as possible, and look in the library for ones unknown.

WHAT TO TALK ABOUT:

Sequencing numbers, matching, ordinal arrangement, plant care.

NURSERY RHYME NUMBERS

WHAT YOU'RE TEACHING:

Number concepts; association of cardinal numbers with number of items they represent

MATERIALS NEEDED:

Nursery rhyme book, a group of twenty-five cards with the numbers one through twenty-five printed on them, a stack of twenty-five cards with one to twenty-five stars stuck on them

WHAT YOU DO:

Read "Little Jack Horner":

> Little Jack Horner,
> Sat in a corner,
> Eating his Christmas pie.
> He stuck in a thumb
> And pulled out a plum,
> And said, "What a good boy am I."

Choose a child to be Jack Horner. Have him sit in the middle of a circle with the deck of object cards. The number cards should be distributed among the other children. Jack should reach into his pie (paper sack), pull out a plum (an object card), and hold it up. The child with the correct number card should hold up the matching card. The first child who fails will become Jack and move to the middle of the circle.

WHAT TO TALK ABOUT:

Talk about counting and matching. Repeat the nursery rhyme. What is a Christmas pie? How many plums would you guess were in Jack's pie?

LISTENING, COUNTING, AND RECORDING

WHAT YOU'RE TEACHING:

Counting, one-to-one correspondence, auditory memory, critical listening

MATERIALS NEEDED:

Butterbean counters, a favorite story, tempera paint, paintbrushes, hair spray

WHAT YOU DO:

Pass out butterbean and other counters. To make butterbean counters, use large, dry white butterbeans. Put down newspapers, and cover with butterbeans (200 or so). Mix tempera paint of assorted colors. Using paintbrushes and taking turns, the children should dab color on the top of each bean. Allow to dry, then spray with hair spray. Make durable, brightly colored markers this way.

Let the children choose a favorite story. Assign each child one letter of the alphabet. Tell the children that while you are reading, you will say, "Go," and when you do they should count every word they hear that begins with their letter and put one counter in a pile. When you say, "Stop," the children should stop and wait for you to say, "Go" again. Do this three or four times during the story.

At the end of the story, the children should count the number of counters they have used. Use this activity several times, and assign different letters to different children so all the children will have a chance to have a popular beginning letter. List the letters on the chalkboard, and allow the children to tally (one mark for each counter) what they count under their letter. Count the tallies.

WHAT TO TALK ABOUT:

We can count letters.

COUNTING FINGERS

WHAT YOU'RE TEACHING:

One-to-one correspondence, creative rhyming

MATERIALS:

Different colored construction paper, pencil, scissors

WHAT YOU DO:

Place your right hand on a stack of five pieces of construction paper, then cut around the outline of your hand. Do the same with the left hand. Cut one finger from one hand, two fingers from the second hand, and three from the next on both hands so that you will have a right and left hand with one through five fingers. By holding up various combinations of these hands, you can represent any number from one through ten.

Present the appropriate number of fingers while you chant the following:

> One, one, start the fun.
> Two, two, I love you.
> Three, three, look at me.
> Four, four, look at the floor.
> Five, five, can you drive?
> Six, six, what a mix!
> Seven, seven, the bread is leaven.
> Eight, eight, shut the gate.
> Nine, nine, watermelon rind.
> Ten, ten, start again.

Repeat the activity, changing the numbers for each child.

WHAT TO TALK ABOUT:

What is rhyming? How does rhyming help us remember? Can you hear rhyme? Think of words that rhyme; write them on the experience chart.

THE LITTLE ENGINE THAT COULD

WHAT YOU'RE TEACHING:

Reinforcing counting, number sequence, cutting skills

MATERIALS NEEDED:

Assorted construction paper, envelopes, felt-tip pens

WHAT YOU DO:

Draw a simple train consisting of an engine and ten box cars. Tell the children you would like each of them to draw an engine and ten box cars and cut them out. Tell them their train can look like yours or their own design.
After the children have finished, take up extra paper and pass out felt-tip pens. Beginning with the first car, have them put the numeral "1" and one dot; on the second, the numeral "2" and two dots, etc. Continue until the last car has the numeral 10 and ten dots. The children should be able to mix up their trains and then put them back together in the correct sequence. (Give help as necessary.) Store the trains in envelopes with the child's name printed on the envelope.

WHAT TO TALK ABOUT:

Sequencing numbers. Has anyone ever counted the cars on a train?

ESTIMATION

- Estimation And Thinking Skills 56
- Patterns And Predictions 57
- Cans Of Sand 58
- Halloween Pumpkin Strips 59
- Estimating Gummy Bits 60
- Thumbs Up/Thumbs Down 61
- The Estimation Game 62
- Watching Things Grow 63

ESTIMATION AND THINKING SKILLS

WHAT YOU'RE TEACHING:

Estimation, comparing, developing thinking skills

MATERIALS NEEDED:

Dry beans, large jar

WHAT YOU DO:

Before the children come to class, put the beans in the jar, place it on a table, and put a large question mark on the jar. Tell the children when they arrive that you were putting beans in a jar and you lost count. Now you do not know how many are in the jar.

Ask the children to guess how many beans they think are in the jar, and write each answer on a piece of paper with each child's name.

Next, let the children help count the number of beans. Let each child count a pile of ten beans until all the beans are in piles of ten. Write down the number of beans, and then reread the estimates the children made. To extend the activity, adapt the game of "May I?" Put a large pile of beans in the middle of the table. One person is "It." "It" asks each child to remove a certain number of beans. When the child is told to get $\underline{X}$ number of beans, the child must remember to say, "May I?" If the child says this, the child may remove that many beans. If the child forgets to say, "May I?" he loses his turn. Continue play until all the beans are gone. Then have children count the number of beans in the individual piles.

WHAT TO TALK ABOUT:

Discuss the difference between guessing and estimating. Ask each child how he decided his estimated guess.

PATTERNS AND PREDICTIONS

WHAT YOU'RE TEACHING:

Recognizing and reproducing patterns, prediction

MATERIALS NEEDED:

Flannel board, felt shapes, colored chalk, poster board, dried peas, dried corn, glue, paper

WHAT YOU DO:

Using the flannel board and shapes, construct a pattern. Ask the children what a pattern is. Have each child try to duplicate the pattern. (Leave the flannel board out with the shapes for the children to use on their own when they have time.)
On the poster board, draw two patterns using circles, squares, and triangles. Put the poster board on the chalk ledge, and call on volunteers to duplicate your pattern on the chalkboard with colored chalk. (Be sure each child gets a turn.) Finally, divide the children into pairs, and demonstrate how to make a pattern using peas and corn. Give each pair of children peas, corn, glue, and 6 inch strips of paper. Challenge the pairs to make their own patterns by gluing on the peas and corn. When each pair has made a pattern, the teacher may help trim the paper and glue the ends together to make a bracelet. Or, glue the strip to heavy paper, and wrap with plastic wrap to make a bookmark.

WHAT TO TALK ABOUT:

Can the children see patterns in their environment? Do plants have leaf patterns? Why is it important to be able to see patterns? (It helps us predict what happens next.)

CANS OF SAND

WHAT YOU'RE TEACHING:

Demonstrate more than and less than, estimation, prediction

MATERIALS NEEDED:

Different sized cans — tall, short, wide, narrow; large sheets of paper for charting, sand

WHAT YOU DO:

Put the cans in the sand. Choose two cans, and have the children predict which can will hold the most. Chart the number of predictions on a large piece of paper. Fill one can with sand, then pour it into the other can. Make statements about one can holding more than or less than another. Continue until all the cans have been filled and all predictions charted. Leave the cans in the sand area so the children can use them as they play.

WHAT TO TALK ABOUT:

More than, less than, predictions, estimations, charting

HALLOWEEN PUMPKIN STRIPS

WHAT YOU'RE TEACHING:

Counting, estimation, number concepts

MATERIALS NEEDED:

Pumpkin, knife, 5 inch black strips of construction paper, felt-tip marker, glue

WHAT YOU DO:

First cut and use your pumpkin for a jack-o'-lantern. After Halloween is over, set your pumpkin on a table covered with newspaper and say, "I wonder how many seeds are inside this pumpkin." Encourage each child to estimate how many seeds are in the pumpkin.

Cut the pumpkin open in several places, and let the children dig out the seeds. Have them place the seeds on newspaper so they can dry overnight. The next day, pass out 5 inch black strips of construction paper. Number at the top of all the strips a number from one to ten.

Put glue and a pile of seeds on each table, and let the children glue on pumpkin seeds to correspond with the number written on the strip of paper.

After the children are finished, the class will have many number concept strips. These can be laminated or covered with plastic wrap. Encourage the children to match the like strips to make sets of one, two, three, etc.

Finally count the seeds and record the number while the children see how many seeds were in the pumpkin from counting the strips.

How close were the children with their estimates? (The strips can be used on a bulletin board for awhile.)

WHAT TO TALK ABOUT:

Talk about the importance of estimation, making sets, number concept strips

ESTIMATING GUMMY BITS

WHAT YOU'RE TEACHING:

Counting, estimation, patterns, graphing, color recognition

MATERIALS NEEDED:

Several packages of gummy bears, a plastic sandwich bag for each child, colored chalk, paper

WHAT YOU DO:

Put at least ten gummy bears into each sandwich bag. Be sure to mix the colors. Give each child a bag of candy.
   a. Divide the children into pairs.
   b. Let each child estimate how many of his favorite color is in the bag. Record the answers and count.
   c. One child should make a color pattern, and his partner should copy the pattern.
   d. Draw a pattern with colored chalk on the board and let the children try and duplicate the pattern.
   e. Draw different colored spots on the board to represent the flavors of the gummy bears. Have children choose their favorite flavor and put them in lines accordingly.
   f. Point out to the children that they have formed a human graph and will copy this on paper so they can study it.
   g. Finally, each child should choose his favorite color and find items in the classroom that are the same color.

(Put each child's name on a bag of candy so each can take a bag.)

WHAT TO TALK ABOUT:

How are colors used to represent flavors? (Yellow is the color of a lemon.) Talk about estimating and graphing answers. Why do we use a graph? (It helps us see a lot of information at a glance.)

THUMBS UP/THUMBS DOWN

WHAT YOU'RE TEACHING:

Numeral recognition, estimation

MATERIALS NEEDED:

A set of dominoes, twelve index cards numbered from one to twelve

WHAT YOU DO:

Gather the children into a group to play "Thumbs Up/Thumbs Down." First, show them one of the numbered cards. Next, briefly show them a domino. If the children think the domino has the same number of dots as the number on the card, they should show the "thumbs up" sign. If not, they should show the "thumbs down" sign.
As the children develop math skills, replace the numbered cards with word cards.
(This activity could also be used with estimating the ingredients during a cooking activity.)

WHAT TO TALK ABOUT:

Why is it important to be able to predict or estimate?

THE ESTIMATION GAME

WHAT YOU'RE TEACHING:

Using a balance scale, weight concepts, vocabulary, estimation

MATERIALS NEEDED:

Simple balance scale; a variety of objects small enough to be used with the scale such as rocks, fruits, erasers, etc.

WHAT YOU DO:

Show the children how the balance scale is used. Demonstrate how an item weighs more or less than another.
After the children have become familiar with the scale and what it does, play "The Estimation Game." Sit with a box containing all the items to be weighed. Remove two objects from the box, and call on one child to estimate which one weighs more and which weighs less. After the child makes his estimation, write it on the chalkboard. Allow the child to weigh the two objects using the balance scale. The child should then tell the class which item weighed more and which weighed less in complete sentences.

WHAT TO TALK ABOUT:

How the balance scale works, other types of scales, why estimation is important, why some things weigh more than others.

WATCHING THINGS GROW

WHAT YOU'RE TEACHING:

Plants become larger as they grow; we can measure and weigh things and record their growth; predicting

MATERIALS NEEDED:

Three petunia bedding plants, three flowerpots filled with soil, poster board, markers, ruler or tape measure, scales, a picture of a petunia (or other bedding plants)

WHAT YOU DO:

Bring in the petunia plants and put them on the table. Encourage the children to examine them along with a picture of a petunia. Divide the poster board into three sets of 3 inch squares. Designate the sets of squares by using different colored markers for each set of squares. Label squares "Week 1," "Week 2," and so on. Inside each square put the words "LENGTH" and "WEIGHT."
Using three identical flowerpots and soil, plant the bedding plants one to a pot. Take a vote among the children to see what color they think each petunia will be. Write the color on the pot. With a ruler or a tape measure, measure each plant from where it enters the soil to the top and record on poster board. Weigh each plant, pot and all, and record the weight in the appropriate square on the poster board. Keep the plants in a well-lighted area and supply water weekly. Each week just before watering, measure and weigh each plant, and record in the appropriate square. When the plants bloom, measure the blooms by laying the ruler across the top and then measure the diameter.

WHAT TO TALK ABOUT:

Do all plants grow the same amount each week? Do all plants grow at the same rate? Do plants increase in weight as they grow? Since the only thing we have added is water, what makes them weigh more? Is this what happens in vegetable gardens?

63

MEASUREMENT

- Measuring And Eating 66
- Spring Sprouts 67
- Measuring With "Feet" 68
- Big Measuring Day 69
- Whose Shirt Is This? 70
- Predicting And Comparing 71
- Bean Potpourri 72
- Cotton Swab Measuring 73
- Do Things Change Size? 74
- Wholes Plus A Part 75
- Toothpaste Stretch 76
- Let's Look And Compare 77

MEASURING AND EATING

WHAT YOU'RE TEACHING:

Developing measuring skills, exploring social aspects of mealtimes, using a ruler, writing numbers practice

MATERIALS NEEDED:

Ruler, string, table knife, fork, spoon, napkins, construction paper (for place mats), pencils, small place for each child

WHAT YOU DO:

Read a book to the children that contains an illustration of a family or group of people eating a meal. Discuss manners, etc. Let the children "get ready" to eat by making a place mat and then setting the table for eating. (Show a place setting you drew on a construction paper place mat.)
The children should decorate the borders of their place mats as they desire. After decorating their place mats, let them trace around plates, knives, forks, and spoons (a place setting).
Now tell the children that everybody will get to measure to see if they have the same size plate. Show the children how to lay a string around the circles they drew for the plates and then the teacher should measure the string. Record the measurement on the place mat in inches (this will require teacher assistance). Also measure the knives, forks, and spoons, and record these measurements on their place mats. To extend the activity, display posters of the four basic food groups. Have the children set their places and take turns choosing a food from each group. Allow children to be waitpersons and take orders. Allow the children to draw and write about their favorite foods. Put their creations into booklets made by stapling plain paper into a construction paper cover.

WHAT TO TALK ABOUT:

The proper place for eating utensils. Why we use them. How to measure a circle.

SPRING SPROUTS

WHAT YOU'RE TEACHING:

Comparing, observing, measuring, math vocabulary

MATERIALS NEEDED:

Ball of string, scissors, dress-up clothes corner, paper strips

WHAT YOU DO:

This is a good activity for springtime when new growth can be seen on trees, bushes, and other plants. Discuss growth with the children. How does their growth differ from plants? How is it similar? (Some children grow faster than others, but everybody usually catches up. However, since everybody is different, we are all shapes and sizes.)

Line up the children according to height with the tallest first along the chalkboard. Have the children put their backs to the chalkboard and draw a line down from the tallest to the shortest. Discuss the differences in height.

Continue your discussion about size. Have the largest child and the smallest child exchange coats. Why don't they fit?

Have the children pair up and let them take turns lying down on the floor while another child measures the one on the floor with a piece of string. Then let the child cut the string and give it to the one being measured.

Take the children, strings, and some strips of paper to the playground. Let the children try and find something the same size as they are as well as something smaller and larger.

Have the children find a plant with new growth (leaves, etc.). Let them measure a leaf with a strip of paper and tear it the same size as the leaf. Let them measure other sprouting leaves to see if they are the same size.

WHAT TO TALK ABOUT:

How things get larger. Do things ever grow smaller? How many ways can we measure things?

MEASURING WITH "FEET"

WHAT YOU'RE TEACHING:

To learn there are many different ways to measure

MATERIALS NEEDED:

Rulers, construction paper, pencils, scissors

WHAT YOU DO:

Tell the children rulers measure what is called "standard English measure."
Let each child draw around his foot on a piece of construction paper and cut it out. Let them measure their feet, tables, books, desks, etc., with a ruler. Record their measurements.

WHAT TO TALK ABOUT:

How rulers help us measure things.

BIG MEASURING DAY

WHAT YOU'RE TEACHING:

Simple measurement, measurement concepts, plant growth

MATERIALS NEEDED:

A styrofoam cup for each child, soil, lima bean seeds, string, rulers

WHAT YOU DO:

Let the children plant a bean seed to see if it will grow.
Give children a styrofoam cup, and help them fill their cups with soil. Children should plant two or three bean seeds in their cups. Have them write their names on the cup. Water the plants frequently, and keep them on a window ledge if possible.
After the beans start to grow, mark a date on the calendar two weeks in the future, and tell the children that day will be the measuring day for the beans! Mark the days off on the calendar. When you finally measure the beans, the children should discover that the bean vines are curved and difficult to measure with a ruler. Ask the children how they could measure them. If no one comes up with a suggestion, explain to the children that they can use string! Lay it beside the vine, curving where necessary, and then lay the string on a ruler to figure the length of the vine. Let each child try measuring his plant! To extend the activity, read *Jack and the Beanstalk*. Allow the children to act out the story. Let the children draw or write about what they did with their bean seeds or the story of *Jack and the Beanstalk*. Also soak some beans. Cut them open, and let the children look at the inside of the beans with a magnifying glass.

WHAT TO TALK ABOUT:

What beans need to grow. Different ways to measure. What's inside a bean that helps it grow?

WHOSE SHIRT IS THIS?

WHAT YOU'RE TEACHING:

Concept of size, math vocabulary, human growth concepts, age concepts

MATERIALS NEEDED:

A wide variety of pairs of different objects reflecting many different age groups, such as shoes, pants, dresses, socks, shirts; blocks, new and used crayons; rocks; leaves

WHAT YOU DO:

Put the clothing on one table and items from the environment on the other. Ask the children to match the various pieces of clothing, e.g., make a pair of socks.

Discuss an item of clothing, e.g., shirts, and how shirts are similar and different (the material could be the same, the sizes different). Talk about why we have different sizes. Where is the size indicated on a shirt? Discuss how our growth affects our clothes size.

As the children pair and group like items of different sizes, discuss why they are different sizes. (The crayons may be different sizes because one has been used and the other has not.) Small acorns may come from a young, small oak tree while larger acorns may come from an old oak tree. Rocks could be different sizes because they are made from different materials, or maybe one was broken. Discuss more size comparisons.

WHAT TO TALK ABOUT:

Discuss how size is one way to determine the differences between objects. Talk about how some things are larger and some smaller. Discuss how things can be the same except for size. Discuss that some children are larger and some smaller. (Emphasize how being large or being small is only one difference between people; neither is good or bad.)

70

PREDICTING AND COMPARING

WHAT YOU'RE TEACHING:

Comparing items, predicting

MATERIALS NEEDED:

Normal classroom or household items brought by the children. All items should be small enough to be picked up. Poster board, markers, and a small balance scale are other materials needed.

WHAT YOU DO:

Line the poster board with three vertical lines and many horizontal lines. Talk to the children about "lighter than" and "heavier than." Discuss meaning and allow children to practice with different items saying, e.g., "This pencil is lighter than this book." Gather a large group of small items together and show the children the poster board labeled "PREDICTION," "HEAVIER," and "LIGHTER." Let each child choose two items and guess which one is heavier and which is lighter. Tell the children to say their prediction in a complete sentence like the example. Write the item chosen as the heaviest in the "PREDICTION" column. Then put the two items on the balance scale. Write the name of the heaviest item in the "HEAVIER" column and the lightest item in the "LIGHTER" column.

WHAT TO TALK ABOUT:

Talk about predicting and the clues we use in determining our answers, for example our senses. Discuss "lighter" and "heavier," also "faster" and "slower," "higher" and "lower", etc., and what they mean.

BEAN POTPOURRI

WHAT YOU'RE TEACHING:

Measuring, classification and sorting, tasting, predicting

MATERIALS NEEDED:

Dried lima beans, blackeyed peas, white beans; small plastic bags; paper towels; plastic cups; soil; crayons; paper; a can of lima beans, a can of blackeyed peas, a can of white beans; markers, ruler; plastic spoons; paper plates

WHAT YOU DO:

Have a bean potpourri. Put two of each kind of bean in three small plastic sacks with wet towels and staple to the bulletin board. Observe the differences as they sprout. Plant three different beans in three plastic cups, add soil, put in a sunny place, and keep them watered. Let the children predict how many of the three different kinds of beans in the cups will grow, and write it on the cup. Write the words "Lima Beans," "Blackeyed Peas," and "White Beans" on the board; give each child three empty cups and a cup of assorted beans. Have the children label the cups, sort, and classify their beans. Later as the bean and pea plants grow, have the children measure the plants.
Open the cans of beans, warm them, and place them in front of the growing plants. Let the children taste each kind of bean.

WHAT TO TALK ABOUT:

How different beans look alike and different. What it takes to grow a bean. Different sizes and colors of beans. How beans and peas compare in taste.

COTTON SWAB MEASURING

WHAT YOU'RE TEACHING:

Understanding nonstandard measuring, comparing sizes, math vocabulary

MATERIALS NEEDED:

Four cotton swabs for each child, colored markers, paper clips.

WHAT YOU DO:

Pass out the cotton swabs, colored markers, and the paper clips. Allow the children to color their cotton swabs any color(s) they choose.

Have the children place two swabs end-to-end. Next, have them line up twelve paper clips end-to-end next to the swabs. Which is longer? Shorter? Allow the children to experiment with their rows of swabs and paper clips. Can they make equal lines?

Have the children measure a large unit block first with swabs, then with paper clips. Record all answers to measurement, e.g., "The block is seven swabs across and also eighteen clips across."

WHAT TO TALK ABOUT:

How many different things can we use to measure? Why do we generally use rulers with inches? Are paper clips just as good?

DO THINGS CHANGE SIZE?

WHAT YOU'RE TEACHING:

Demonstrating that moving an object from one place to another does not change its size; nonstandard measurement

MATERIALS NEEDED:

Two yardsticks, two branches from a small tree both (the same size but not 36 inches), several brand new pencils

WHAT YOU DO:

Place the yardsticks on the floor a short distance apart with the ends even; do the same with the branches. Ask the children if they are the same size. Next, put the pairs beside each other, only this time have one of each pair beginning at a different point than the other so the ends will not be aligned. Now ask the children if the pairs of objects are the same size. If the children say, "No," have them measure the pairs with new pencils to see if they are the same "pencil lengths long."
Choose two children; let one hold a yardstick and one a branch. Have the children stand by a window. Choose two other children, one to hold the other yardstick and one to hold the other branch. Have the children take the items outside, and let them see one of each pair at a distance and one upclose. Now, which one is longer?
If the children think the one that looks shorter (due to the distance the item is away from the children) is really shorter, have the children measure again to see if the length has actually changed.

WHAT TO TALK ABOUT:

Why do things look like they change sizes? Do they really change sizes? How can we find out if things change sizes? What can we use to measure?

74

WHOLES PLUS A PART

WHAT YOU'RE TEACHING:

Measuring wholes plus a part, nonstandard measuring

MATERIALS NEEDED:

Bottle caps all the same size, an eraser, pencils, paper, other small items from the classroom

WHAT YOU DO:

Have the children choose an item and estimate how many bottle caps long the item is. Help the children record their estimations with pencils and paper. Place the item(s) to be measured on a table beginning at one edge. Line up the bottle caps next to the item(s), again beginning at the edge of the table. Children should discover that some items are an exact number of bottle caps and some items may be between a certain number (more than five but not all of six, i.e., between five and six). Compare the estimation to the actual size.

WHAT TO TALK ABOUT:

Talk about the length of the objects. Is the length closer to, for example, five or six bottle caps? How would you tell someone else how long the object was? Could you say, "Almost six bottle caps long?" Or, say, "A little more than five bottle caps long?"

TOOTHPASTE STRETCH

WHAT YOU'RE TEACHING:

Measuring, estimating, alternative ways of measuring

MATERIALS NEEDED:

Two small tubes of different brands of toothpaste with the same ounces, butcher paper, string, ruler

WHAT YOU DO:

Bring in two small tubes of different brands of toothpaste the same size. Let the children examine them. Ask them if they think each tube has the same amount of toothpaste in it. Ask the children if they know a way to find out. Discuss answers and suggestions. Use two 10 foot strips of butcher paper. Lay them on the floor side-by-side. Draw a line for a starting point on each piece of paper.

Beginning at the starting line, let the children take turns squeezing the tubes, always from the bottom, to lay a strip of toothpaste up and down the butcher paper until the tube is empty. Using string, lay the string along the side of the strip of toothpaste, being careful to follow all turns. Do this with both strips of toothpaste. Measure the string used to determine which tube had the most toothpaste.

WHAT TO TALK ABOUT:

What are some of the reasons one tube may actually have more toothpaste? (Thickness of the toothpaste, how it is made.) Why may it seem to have more? (The way the tube was squeezed, e.g., squeezed too hard several times making the strip lumpy.)

LET'S LOOK AND COMPARE

WHAT YOU'RE TEACHING:

Becoming familiar with metric measure, comparing liters and quarts

MATERIALS NEEDED:

Empty liter cold drink bottles, pint bottles, quart bottles, gallon milk bottles, supply of sand

WHAT YOU DO:

Using a sand table inside or a sandbox, observe the differences between pints, liters, quarts, and gallons. Encourage the children to fill different containers with sand and pour it from one container into another. Help the children discover:

    Which is more, a quart or a liter?
    How many pints are in a quart?
    How many pints are in a liter?
    How many liters are in a quart?
    How many quarts are in a gallon?
    How many liters are in a gallon?

WHAT TO TALK ABOUT:

Talk about the differences between liters and quarts. Why are soft drinks packaged in liters?

MONEY AND TIME

- Buried Treasure 80
- Chain Of Days 81
- Playing With Time 82
- How Much Is It? 83

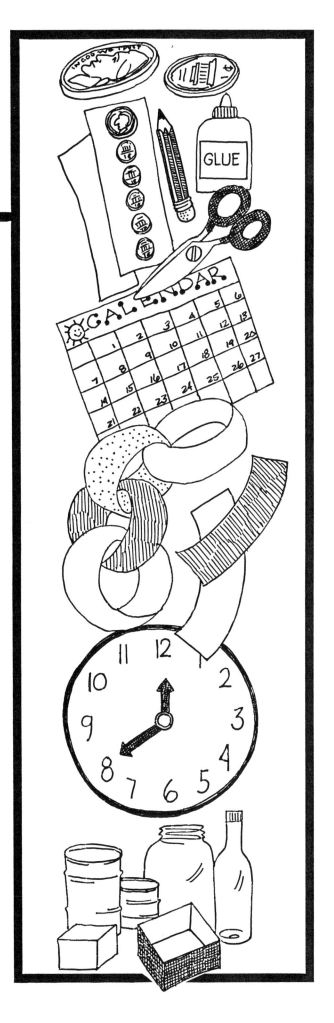

BURIED TREASURE

WHAT YOU'RE TEACHING:

Recognizing coins, coin values, counting

MATERIALS NEEDED:

Three dollars in pennies, three dollars in nickels, outside sand area or an area of soft soil, construction paper, plastic wrap

WHAT YOU DO:

While value is a concept that develops slowly in young children, beginning recognition and exposure to value should begin simply and early. Most young children have little difficulty recognizing pennies and and nickels, but most do not understand their values. Play a swap game in the classroom. Give some of the children five pennies and some a nickel. Discuss the values and have children count and swap pennies for nickels.

Make coin strips (use same procedure as pea strips on page 57). Use a strip of cardboard divided into six sections. Glue a nickel in the top section and glue five pennies in a row down from the nickel. Wrap in plastic wrap. Allow the children to handle and use the coin strips in the classroom.

Some time during the day (or at the end of the day for use the next day) let one child take the pennies to the sand area. Bury them in a small area not too deep. Let the children go on a treasure hunt to dig up and find as many pennies as they can. Instruct children to see how many nickels worth of pennies they can find. Let the children swap their pennies for nickels. At the end of the activity, gather the coins for later use.

WHAT TO TALK ABOUT:

The value of different coins. How many pennies are in a nickel? What materials are pennies made from? Nickels? (Pennies are made from zinc plated with copper; nickels are made from nickel.)

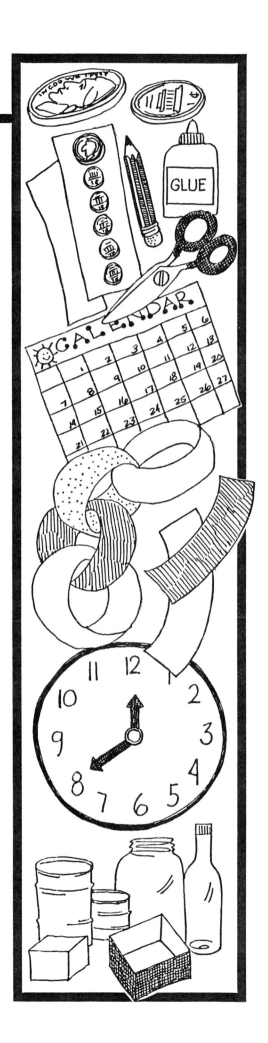

CHAIN OF DAYS

WHAT YOU'RE TEACHING:

Simple subtraction, counting, time concepts

MATERIALS NEEDED:

Different colored construction paper, glue, scissors, calendar

WHAT YOU DO:

This activity is good for any holiday or other special event that will be celebrated at school. The teacher should share a calendar with the children. Identify the day (holiday or event), and then count the number of days left until that day.
Have the children cut the construction paper in half and then cut the halves into 1 inch strips. Help them prepare a chain by gluing the ends of one paper strip together. Then put the next piece through the paper ring and glue the ends of that paper strip together. Continue until the chain has the same number of links as the number of days left in the month. Each day a child can tear one ring off the chain and then count how many days are left. (Mondays are fun because students get to tear off three rings!)

WHAT TO TALK ABOUT:

Holidays, simple subtraction, days of the week

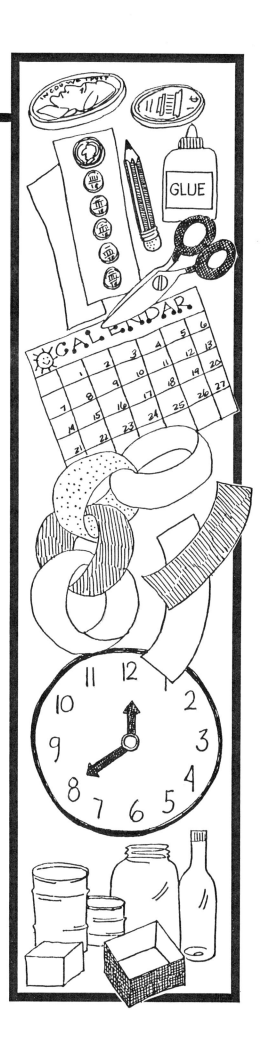

PLAYING WITH TIME

WHAT YOU'RE TEACHING:

Introducing time concepts, reading numbers

MATERIALS NEEDED:

White construction paper, felt-tip pens, large clockface (commercial or teacher-made), brads, wall clock, black construction paper

WHAT YOU DO:

This activity can be used for introducing time.
For an art activity, allow the children to make clockfaces. Use a 12 inch circle of white construction paper, and help the children write on the numbers using the play clock or wall clock as a model. Help the children cut two hands for their clock from black construction paper. Punch a hole in the center of the circle and the bottom of the hands, and fasten the hands to the clock with brads so the hands will move.
Using the clock displayed on the chalk ledge, set the clock for the time a certain event will take place such as recess or snack time, and help the children set their clocks for the same time. Say to the children, "I have set my clock for 10 o'clock, and that is when we will have our snack. Look at the clock on the wall. It does not show 10 o'clock yet. I want you to watch the wall clock, and when it gets to 10 o'clock, it will look just like your clocks. When you see the wall clock look like yours, hold up your hands because it will then be 10 o'clock and time for a snack."
(Using this activity during the year will develop time concepts.)

WHAT TO TALK ABOUT:

Time — the past and future; times when we eat, go to school, sleep; why it is important to know the time.

HOW MUCH IS IT?

WHAT YOU'RE TEACHING:

The value of money, identifying money, buying concepts, counting, social study awareness

MATERIALS NEEDED:

Empty cans, packages, containers, and boxes in which food was packaged; empty milk and other drink cartons; pennies; markers; pencils; stickers; newspapers

WHAT YOU DO:

Move shelves and tables to one section of the classroom, and arrange the furniture to resemble a small grocery store. Help the children arrange the groceries in like groups putting vegetables, drinks, and other like foods together. Explain to the children that most of their parents look at the prices to find out how much they cost and to plan their food budgets. Let the children look through grocery ads in the newspapers to see if they can find the prices they should put on their groceries. Help the children price the groceries with markers.

Allow two or three children to be workers in the store and the remaining to be customers in the store.

Small groups of children, with the teacher's help, should make out a short grocery list and shop at the store. Have them pay pennies. (If pennies are in short supply, help the children make pennies from brown construction paper.)

As time passes, nickels, dimes, quarters, half-dollars, and dollars may be used for money as the children become more proficient.

WHAT TO TALK ABOUT:

Family needs (food), stores, why they sell food, where the grocer gets the food to sell, and a variety of similar concepts.

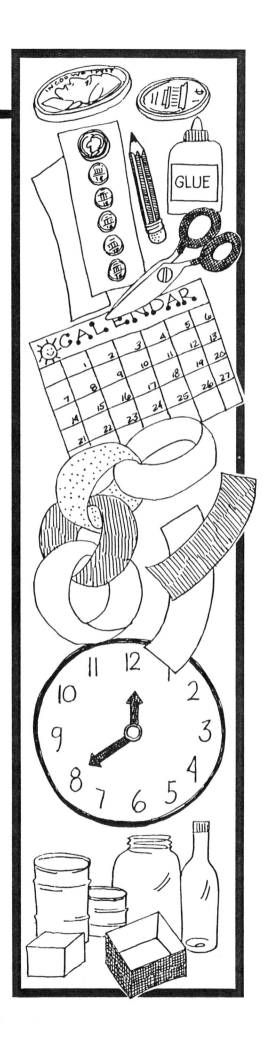

ORDINAL NUMBERS

- "Ordering" A Hamburger...........86
- Ordinal Sandwiches 87
- Ordering The Ordinals..............88
- Ghosts And Ordinal Numbers...89
- Ordinal Balloons 90
- What Is Missing?.....................91

"ORDERING" A HAMBURGER

WHAT YOU'RE TEACHING:

Ordering, recognizing numbers, self-expression

MATERIALS NEEDED:

Assorted construction paper, marker, scissors.
Use light brown construction paper for hamburger bun:

    black for meat   white for onion
    yellow for cheese   dark brown for bacon
    green for lettuce   red for tomato

WHAT YOU DO:

Provide patterns and have children cut out light brown hamburger buns, black hamburgers, yellow cheese, green lettuce, white onion, red tomatoes, and dark brown bacon. Let them number, with both numerals and dots, the ingredients in order:

    bottom bun 1   meat 4   tomato 7
    lettuce 2   onion 5   top bun 8
    bacon 3   cheese 6

Put the foods together in a serving line on a table. Let the children build their hamburgers by placing the ingredients together by ordering from one to eight.

Let the children cut out ingredients from construction paper that are not represented. (Let the child decide on the color and the proper numerical order for that ingredient.) Let each child tell the class why his hamburger is different.

Have the children staple their hamburgers together to make a hamburger book. Have them write and illustrate a story about their hamburgers.

WHAT TO TALK ABOUT:

Discuss ordering or sequencing and why it is important. Discuss the nutritional aspects of hamburgers.

ORDINAL SANDWICHES

WHAT YOU'RE TEACHING:

Practice using ordinal numbers

MATERIALS NEEDED:

Brown, white, red, yellow, and green construction paper

WHAT YOU DO:

Cut out white bread slices, yellow circles for mustard, red circles for tomato slices, green lettuce, and brown pieces of lunch meat. Number one slice of bread "1," mustard "2," meat "3," tomato "4," lettuce "5," and the second piece of bread "6." Have the children construct sandwiches in small groups. The children should share with group members how they are making their sandwiches. For example, "First, I use a piece of bread; second, I put mustard on my bread; third, I put meat on..." Let them write the ordinal numbers on each sandwich part.

WHAT TO TALK ABOUT:

Is bread always the first part of sandwiches? What is the last item usually put on sandwiches?

87

ORDERING THE ORDINALS

WHAT YOU'RE TEACHING:

Characteristics of ordinal numbers

MATERIALS NEEDED:

Nine styrofoam cups, markers, peanuts, sugarless hard candy, carrot slices, cellophane wrapped pieces of bubble gum, apple chunks, animal crackers, paper pad, pencil

WHAT YOU DO:

Write the ordinal numbers from first to ninth on the styrofoam cups. Put a different snack in each cup. Let the children take turns being the waiter. The waiter should ask, "What may I bring you, sir/ma'am?" The customer should order by saying, "Please bring me a _____ from the fourth cup." The waiter will write the order on the paper pad and bring the correct order to the child.

WHAT TO TALK ABOUT:

Talk about ordinal numbers and how they are different from cardinal numbers.

GHOST AND ORDINAL NUMBERS

WHAT YOU'RE TEACHING:

Ordinal number concepts, writing ordinal numbers, counting

MATERIALS NEEDED:

Five tongue depressors for each child, white construction paper, crayons

WHAT YOU DO:

Teach the children the finger play about the five little ghosts:

Five little ghosts, all dressed in white,
Were scaring each other on Halloween night.
"Boo!" said the **first** one. "I'll catch you!"
"Wooo," said the **second**. "I don't care if you do!"
The **third** ghost said, "You can't run away from me."
The **fourth** one said, "I'll scare everyone I see."
The **fifth** one said, "It's time to disappear. See you at Halloween time next year!"

Let the children make ghosts and act out the finger play. Draw on the blackboard a "generic" ghost of any shape to give the children an idea of what a ghost may look like. Have the children draw five different-looking ghosts on white construction paper and cut them out. Have the children glue each ghost to a tongue depressor. Write the words "First," "Second," "Third," "Fourth," and "Fifth" on the chalkboard, and let the children label each of their ghosts. Help them learn the words of the finger play and hold up their ghosts with the ordinal number as they use it in the play.

WHAT TO TALK ABOUT:

Tell the children that these number words are ordinal number words, and tell which place something belongs. Talk about lining up and the way we count. Discuss being "first" winner in a game.

ORDINAL BALLOONS

WHAT YOU'RE TEACHING:

Ordinal numbers concept, expressive language, math vocabulary

MATERIALS NEEDED:

Ten balloons all the same color, felt-tip marker, cellophane tape

WHAT YOU DO:

Blow up the ten balloons. With a felt-tip marker, number the balloons first through tenth. Tape the balloons to the wall in the math center and arrange them from left to right numerically.

At different times, call upon children to count and call the ordinal numbers. Always go from left to right. Begin slowly, perhaps with only three or four, because this is a very difficult concept for young children.

Encourage children to talk about what they are doing using complete sentences. Example: "This is the third balloon."

WHAT TO TALK ABOUT:

The differences between ordinal numbers and cardinal numbers. What does "first" mean? Second?

WHAT IS MISSING?

WHAT YOU'RE TEACHING:

Missing number in a sequence, ordering pictorial sequencing, solving problems by finding a pattern, higher level thinking skills

MATERIALS NEEDED:

Number cards, paper, crayons, colored chalk, envelopes, scissors

WHAT YOU DO:

Draw shapes on the chalkboard or experience chart following this pattern: triangle; triangle, circle; triangle, circle, square; triangle, circle, square, star. Say to the children, "If I were to make another row and only used circles, how many circles would I draw?" (Four.)
For variation, omit a row and ask how many are missing. Write on the board the numbers one through eight, omitting two and four.
Challenge the children to supply the missing numbers. Practice this activity until the skill is mastered.
Discuss activities the children do on a daily basis like brushing their teeth. Pass out crayons and paper folded into thirds. Have the children draw the first thing they do in the morning in the first third, the second thing they do in the second third, and the last thing they do in the last third. (Do not limit to one activity.)
Have the children cut the three sections apart and put them in an envelope. Children should swap envelopes and put the pictures inside in the correct sequence.

WHAT TO TALK ABOUT:

Patterns, sequencing, numbers and sequencing numbers

SETS

- Making And Recognizing Sets ...94
- Two Of What? 95
- Making Patterns 96
- Combining Like Sets.................97
- Making Sets 98
- My Leg Book............................99
- Apple Trees 100
- Big Blues And Little Yellows....101

MAKING AND RECOGNIZING SETS

WHAT YOU'RE TEACHING:

Recognizing sets, math vocabulary (fewer, smaller, larger, etc.)

MATERIALS NEEDED:

Two boxes of multicolored breakfast cereals, black yarn, newspapers

WHAT YOU DO:

Introduce simple sets to children by explaining that a set is a group of like objects. Show some examples, such as pencils, chalk, and other items from the room.
Put the children in small groups around the room and spread newspapers on the floor for each group. Provide a pile of cereal and yarn for each group. Let the children sort the cereal according to color and surround each group with yarn. Explain that each group is a set of like objects.
Then instruct the children to make smaller sets and make sets with fewer, more, and larger amounts of cereal.

WHAT TO TALK ABOUT:

What is a set? How do we change a set (add or take away). Talk about "math vocabulary," more than, less than, fewer, larger, like sets. What would a set with nothing in it be called? (Empty set.)

TWO OF WHAT?

WHAT YOU'RE TEACHING:

Pair concepts (numbers, similarities and differences)

MATERIALS NEEDED:

Several pairs of items such as, socks, gloves, a pair of pants; pairs other than clothing; a flannel board, cutouts of miscellaneous pairs

WHAT YOU DO:

Discuss pairs with the children. Have them name all the things they can think of that people normally refer to as pairs, such as a pair of shoes. Write all the pairs the children name on the experience chart. Set up a flannel board and demonstrate pairs of objects (including those the children name) on the flannel board. Each time a pair is introduced, count the items and let the children tell how they are alike or different. For example, the two gloves that make a pair are different because of the finger placements. After all the children have participated, put all the items on a table and let the children make pairs.

WHAT TO TALK ABOUT:

Why a pair of pants is called a pair even though it is one item of clothing. Would two different colored socks the same type be a pair? (They could be called a pair of socks or a set of two socks.) A pair of pants, on the other hand, could never be a set of two pants. They could only be a set of two pairs of pants.

MAKING PATTERNS

WHAT YOU'RE TEACHING:

Pattern concepts, problem-solving using manipulatives, classification

MATERIALS NEEDED:

Counters of various sizes and colors, colored chalk, prepared patterns drawn on poster board, markers

WHAT YOU DO:

Seat the children at tables or in groups on the floor. Be sure each group has an ample supply of different kinds and colors of markers. Talk to the children about patterns. Explain it is a design that can be copied. Tell the children you will draw a pattern on the board and then they should copy the pattern using the items and colors you have drawn. Draw several patterns for the children to make.
Divide the children into small groups and let them copy each other's patterns.

WHAT TO TALK ABOUT:

Discuss patterns found in the environment, such as clockfaces, calendars, mealtimes, and other everyday activities.

COMBINING LIKE SETS

WHAT YOU'RE TEACHING:

Practice with sets, counting, combining like sets

MATERIALS NEEDED:

Many plastic counters; or make your own with beans, peas, corn, or other items that have been colored with tempera and allowed to dry; yarn

WHAT YOU DO:

Arrange the children into pairs or three's. Give each group a pile of thirty markers, all the same color. Tell the children you will call out a number and they should make two or three piles of that many and then place a piece of yarn around each pile to make a set.

After the children have arranged some sets, tell them to make three sets and put yarn around each one. Then tell the children to remove the yarn from around two of the sets, combine and count them, and put a piece of yarn around the combined sets. Tell them this is called combining like sets, that you can put like sets together as long as everything is alike.

Next let the children take the yarn from the combined sets and the set they have left. Tell them to put both of their sets together, count them, and put a piece of yarn around them. Now they have one large set made by combining three like sets.

Finally, have the children divide the large set into three like sets, putting a piece of yarn around each.

WHAT TO TALK ABOUT:

Sets, like sets, how we can combine like sets.

MAKING SETS

WHAT YOU'RE TEACHING:

Reinforcement of recognizing numbers, making sets

MATERIALS NEEDED:

A regular deck of playing cards with the face cards removed for upper primary grades; for kindergarten and first graders, make four 5" x 8" sets of cards, each set colored differently and put together for a deck of cards; add one card with the picture of a turkey

WHAT YOU DO:

Three or four children can play at a time. More children can play if the deck of cards is doubled. Each child is dealt five cards, and the rest of the cards should be facedown. Each child must take a card from the deck. If he makes a set of two, the child lays it down. Play is continued until one child is left with the "turkey card."
The teacher should always play the first game with those who have not played before.

WHAT TO TALK ABOUT:

Matching sets, numerals, gamesmanship, rules.

MY LEG BOOK

WHAT YOU'RE TEACHING:

Counting, observation, making sets

MATERIALS NEEDED:

Old newspapers, scissors, glue, pencils, construction paper, magazines

WHAT YOU DO:

Ask the children how many legs they have. Do all creatures have two legs? Let the children cut out pictures of animals, insects, people, fish, or any living thing from their magazines. Each picture should be glued to construction paper.

The children should count the number of legs of each animal, etc., in each picture and write that number on their pictures. Children should be encouraged to make sets of pictures where all the creatures have the same number of legs.

To extend the activity, have the children form sets of legs together. Example: two children would be a set of four, and five children would be a set of ten.

WHAT TO TALK ABOUT:

Discuss the pictures and numbers of legs the creatures have. Discuss reasons for the different numbers of legs. Talk about making sets.

APPLE TREES

WHAT YOU'RE TEACHING:

Constructing sets, following directions, counting

MATERIALS NEEDED:

Flannel board; brown, white, green and red flannel or felt; scissors

WHAT YOU DO:

Prepare in advance a flannel tree trunk, greenery for the top of an apple tree, and numbers one through ten out of felt.

Pass out red felt, and have each child cut out one or two small round circles for apples. Place the felt tree and a felt number on the flannel board. Have a child count the number of apples needed on the tree to match that number. Let the class help you count and check this answer.

After placing the felt apples on the tree, remove them and let another child count a set to match the number you place on the flannel board. Continue this activity until all the sets of numbers, one through ten, have been counted. Let the children use this activity on their own when they have time.

WHAT TO TALK ABOUT:

Discuss making like sets. Talk about sets in the environment: sets of leaves, flowers, etc.

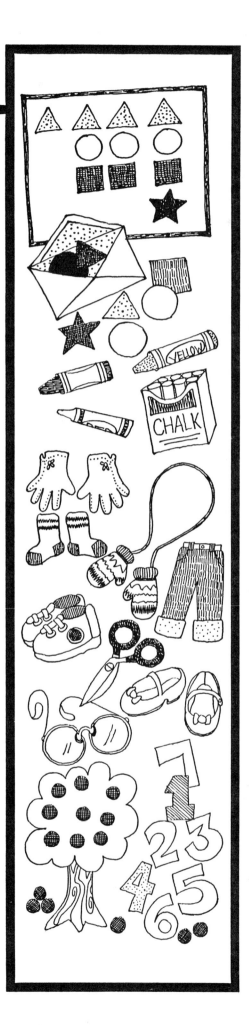

BIG BLUES AND LITTLE YELLOWS

WHAT YOU'RE TEACHING:

Developing concepts about sets, developing an understanding that an object may have more than one feature

MATERIALS NEEDED:

Red, blue, and yellow construction paper; scissors

WHAT YOU DO:

Help the children cut triangles from construction paper. Divide the children into six groups, and have one group cut small red triangles, one group cut large red triangles, one small yellow triangles, one large yellow triangles, the fifth group cut small blue triangles, and the last group cut large blue triangles. Collect all the triangles and mix them up.
Gather the children into a large group on the floor, and pass out one triangle to each child. Explain that each is one color and either large or small.
Tell the children to listen carefully and you will call out names of triangles. If they have that triangle, they should hold it up.
Call out:
> Hold up all large blue triangles.
> Hold up all blue small triangles.
> Hold up all large yellow triangles.
> Hold up all small yellow triangles.
> Hold up all large red triangles.
> Hold up all small red triangles.

WHAT TO TALK ABOUT:

Discuss how something can be described in at least two ways, such as tall and skinny, short and skinny, etc. Let the children give examples.

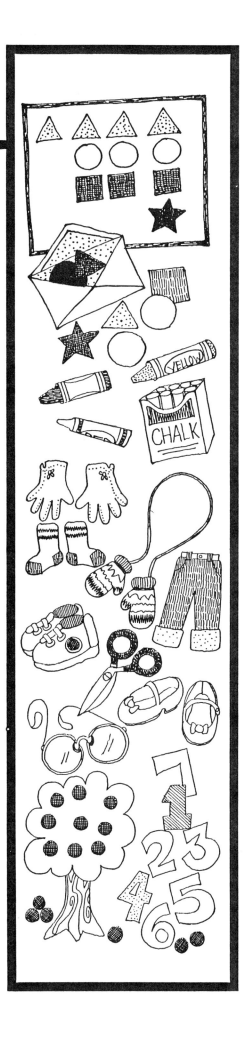

SHAPE AND SIZE

- Wind Chimes 104
- Feed The Shape Box 105
- Freehand, Decorated Shape Necklaces 106
- Counting The Wind 107
- Shapes 108
- Time For Pilgrims Again 109
- Finding Shapes 110
- Making Patterns 111
- Talking Shapes 112
- Simple Shapes 113
- Making Shapes And Eating 114
- Shaping The Outside 115
- Tossing On The Sheet 116
- Math Mobiles 117

WIND CHIMES

WHAT YOU'RE TEACHING:

Comparing length, similarities and differences, planned sequencing

MATERIALS NEEDED:

A coat hanger for each child, brightly colored yarn, variety of different sized nails

WHAT YOU DO:

Give each child a coat hanger and several pieces of colored yarn of various lengths. Let children make wind chimes by tying nails to the end of the yarn tied to the bottom of the coat hanger. (Children should use both lengths of yarn to make the nails uneven so they will hit together at different places on the nails.) The thickness of the nails will also change sounds. (Make sure they use the longest and biggest nails in the center.)

WHAT TO TALK ABOUT:

Why do we put the nails at different lengths? How do we determine the length?

FEED THE SHAPE BOX

WHAT YOU'RE TEACHING:

Circle concepts, square, triangle; shape discrimination

MATERIALS NEEDED:

A medium-sized cardboard box with a triangular hole, a square hole, and a circular hole cut in the side of the box.

WHAT YOU DO:

Show the box to the children pointing out the shape of the holes. Tell them they will play a game called "Feed Me A Shape." Divide the class into two teams. The teams will each form a line. The object of the game is to find something in the room that will go into the matched hole in the box.
To begin, the first child in each line picks out something in the room that will fit in the holes. Continue the game until it is impossible for one child to find a shape that will fit the hole.
To extend the activity, use cookie dough from the grocery store, and form into shapes, circles, squares, and triangles. Bake in a toaster over. Children can then "eat a shape."

WHAT TO TALK ABOUT:

Discuss the attributes and physical description of circles, squares, and triangles.

FREEHAND, DECORATED SHAPE NECKLACES

WHAT YOU'RE TEACHING:

Reinforcement of geometric shapes, creative art, small motor development

MATERIALS NEEDED:

Different colored construction paper, glue, scissors, glitter, crayons, yarn

WHAT YOU DO:

Tell the children that everyone will make a shape (square, circle, triangle, or rectangle) necklace or other decoration. Pass out construction paper, scissors, glue, glitter, and yarn. Tell the children to draw squares, triangles, circles, and rectangles on a sheet of construction paper. After the children have filled a page with shapes, have them lay their papers with the shapes against a blank sheet of paper so that when they cut out their shapes, they will have two alike.

After the children finish cutting, they should gather and put their shapes together. Show the children how to put a drop of glue at the top and bottom of the shapes to stick them together leaving a space between the pairs of shapes.

Then let the children decorate their shapes with crayons, glitter, and glue. After the shapes have dried, show them how to thread the yarn to make necklaces or bracelets. Let the children create other decorations if they wish.

WHAT TO TALK ABOUT:

How shapes are alike and different. Compare large shapes with smaller shapes. Count sides and corners. How is the circle different?

COUNTING THE WIND

WHAT YOU'RE TEACHING:

Moving air causes wind, and the faster it moves, the harder it blows. Charting, counting.

MATERIALS NEEDED:

Sack of beans, paper, felt-tip pens, glue, plastic wrap

WHAT YOU DO:

Using paper, beans, and glue, help the children construct wind counters. On the first piece of paper, glue one bean and write the number "1" and put one dot. On the second piece of paper, glue two beans, write the number "2" and put two dots. Continue this until you have beans, numbers, and dots on ten pieces of paper. Using plastic wrap, laminate the papers.
Let the children handle the papers so they can see that the weight of the paper depends on the number of beans. On a breezy day, move a table outside and lay the wind counters on the table. See how many of the papers blow off the table. If the wind, for example, is strong enough to blow the first six papers off the table, it could be said that the wind is "six beans strong." Put the papers out every day for a week or longer and record how hard the wind blows. By using the clock and noting the times the papers blow off, it can be possible to see if the wind blows harder at certain times of the day.

WHAT TO TALK ABOUT:

What causes wind? Does the wind blow harder at certain times of the day? The year? Are there other ways to measure the wind? Use a weather vane. Discuss how we "use" the wind.

SHAPES

WHAT YOU'RE TEACHING:

Learning shapes, small motor control

MATERIALS NEEDED:

Potatoes; carrots; turnips; squares, circles, triangles, and rectangles cut from different colored felt; felt board; masking tape; wooded circles, squares, triangles, and rectangles; finger paint or thick tempera paint; white paper; plastic knives

WHAT YOU DO:

Using the felt board, show the four different shapes to the children by putting one square, two circles, three rectangles, and four triangles on the board. Let different children count the shapes, calling out the names as they do so. Rearrange the order. (Example: use one circle for one square and two squares for two circles and other arrangements.)

Prepare in advance by cutting a potato in half. Use the flat side of the potato and cut away the potato to leave a circle, a triangle, and a square. Do the same with half a carrot and half a turnip. Let the children use their plastic knives to try and duplicate the shapes you made. Put out trays of finger paint or tempera paint, dip the vegetables into the paint, and print the shapes on white paper.

Make large shapes on the floor with masking tape. Instruct the children to march around the shapes. They can use their arms and legs in other activities that will allow a spatial view and an understanding of shapes.

WHAT TO TALK ABOUT:

What determines what a shape looks like? (The outside lines.) Name shapes in the room and their environment. Are there shapes that do not have names?

TIME FOR PILGRIMS AGAIN

WHAT YOU'RE TEACHING:

Shape recognition, creative thinking

MATERIALS NEEDED:

Glue; white and black construction paper shapes; circles, rectangles, squares, and triangles of all sizes; manila paper

WHAT YOU DO:

When Thanksgiving approaches, include making pilgrims as a part of the activity. Give the children an assortment of shapes and ask them to put together paper pilgrims from their collection of black and white shapes.

WHAT TO TALK ABOUT:

Discuss the pilgrim's role in the first Thanksgiving. Talk about their clothing and how/why it was mostly black and white.

FINDING SHAPES

WHAT YOU'RE TEACHING:

Learning shape names, creative art

MATERIALS NEEDED:

Twenty-five each of circles, squares, triangles, and rectangles; construction paper; glue; felt-tip pens

WHAT YOU DO:

Discuss with the children how we see shapes everywhere in the environment. ("A door is shaped as a rectangle," could be an example.)
Pass out the shapes, construction paper, pens, and glue. Explain that you would like them to combine the cutout shapes to form a picture(s) of something in their environment. Felt-tip pens can be used for drawing details. Children should name their picture(s) and list the shapes used.

WHAT TO TALK ABOUT:

How much of nature is "made" by various shapes?

MAKING PATTERNS

WHAT YOU'RE TEACHING:

Learning shape names, creativity, following directions

MATERIALS NEEDED:

A large number of different colored plastic pushpins, a 5" x 5" piece of cardboard for each child, chalk, blank paper, pencils

WHAT YOU DO:

Give each child a piece of cardboard and several pushpins. Allow the children to "play" with the materials as they observe them. Give each child a piece of plain blank paper, and be sure they all have pencils. Tell the children you will make shapes on the board using dots made from chalk and write the name of the shape.
Let the children duplicate the shape on their cardboard pieces and write the name of the shape on a separate piece of paper with a pencil drawing of it. Later, the children should be encouraged to make up "new" shapes and name them.

WHAT TO TALK ABOUT:

Similarities and differences; things in the room and environment that are the same shapes the children made.

TALKING SHAPES

WHAT YOU'RE TEACHING:

Learning shapes, characteristics of different shapes

MATERIALS NEEDED:

Tongue depressors; construction paper; glue; felt-tip pens; patterns for a circle, square, triangle, and rectangle; scissors

WHAT YOU DO:

Help each child cut out a circle, triangle, square, and rectangle. Let them glue each shape to a tongue depressor. The children can draw faces on their shapes and give them a name if they desire.
Let different children hold up a shape and tell the class all about it. For example: "This is a triangle. It has three sides and three corners."
Let the class make up stories with their shapes as the main characters. Let children write stories about their shapes.

WHAT TO TALK ABOUT:

Talk about the characteristics of shapes. What could be constructed using shapes (person, car, etc.)?

SIMPLE SHAPES

WHAT YOU'RE TEACHING:

Recognition of shapes, use of shapes, creative art

MATERIALS NEEDED:

Construction paper shapes: squares, circle, triangles, rectangles of many sizes; manila paper; flannel board; flannel board cutouts of the shapes

WHAT YOU DO:

Set up your flannel board and two shapes. Discuss the similarities and differences pointing out sides, angles, straight lines, and curved lines. Add one shape at a time until children are discussing all four.

Pass out piles of shapes to tables where you have grouped your children. Put out glue and manila paper. Tell the children to see what kind of pictures they can make by gluing the shapes on manila paper. After they have finished, let the groups share what they have done. Volunteers can show what they have made to the class and tell what it is or tell a story about their pictures. To extend the activity, encourage the children to make shape books. Help each child make a book by folding a piece of construction paper over two blank pieces of paper, and staple at the fold. Let the children glue a different shape on each page and draw a shape picture with crayons using the shape as part of the picture.

WHAT TO TALK ABOUT:

How the different shapes are alike and different. How things in the environment are made of shapes. Point out things in the classroom that are square, circular, or seem to be made of rectangles or triangles.

MAKING SHAPES AND EATING

WHAT YOU'RE TEACHING:

Construction and naming two-dimensional shapes

MATERIALS NEEDED:

Foods children like to eat that can be served as snacks, such as popcorn, peanuts, celery sticks, carrot slices, vanilla wafers, dry cereal; paper plates

WHAT YOU DO:

Divide the children into groups, and pass out one paper plate per child. Pass out snack materials, and tell the children to wait to eat.

Draw a circle on the board and challenge them to duplicate the circle on their paper plate using their snack food. After they have made the circle, ask them to eat some of the outside. Is it still a circle (or name of other shape)? Repeat this activity using a square, triangle, and rectangle.

WHAT TO TALK ABOUT:

Discuss similarities and differences between the circle, square, triangle, and rectangle. Discuss how the shape is determined by the outside line.

SHAPING THE OUTSIDE

WHAT YOU'RE TEACHING:

Understanding shape concepts

MATERIALS NEEDED:

Assorted real objects such as a jar lid, playing cards, puzzle pieces, shoe box top, index card, paper, pencils, crayons

WHAT YOU DO:

Too often we assume young children know what a particular word means. "Trace a shape" has no real meaning, yet children learn to trace with sometimes no concept of shape. Tell children that "shape" is the line around the outside of something.

Put children in groups and pass out objects for the children to trace around the outside. After tracing, let them name the shapes. (This is a good activity early in the year.)

Children can trace geometric shapes after they master simple shapes. Then see if they can find geometric shapes in the environment.

WHAT TO TALK ABOUT:

How the line around or on the outside determines shape. Things in the environment that have geometric shape.

115

TOSSING ON THE SHEET

WHAT YOU'RE TEACHING:

Learning shapes, small motor development, eye/hand coordination

MATERIALS NEEDED:

An old sheet; large scraps of cloth; beans, corn, or pea gravel; large-eyed needles; thread; four different colors of tempera paint; brushes; scissors

WHAT YOU DO:

Mix four different colors of tempera paint. Help the children outline several different shapes on the sheet (circles, squares, triangles, and rectangles). Let the children paint the shapes with tempera paint.
Pass out the cloth, beans, corn, or pea gravel, and helping with measuring, have the children cut out 5 inch squares.
Then let the children thread the large-eyed needles. Let them have two squares and sew three sides together leaving the fourth unsewn.
Next, the children should put a small amount of the filler they have inside the sewn pocket and sew the fourth side to make a beanbag.
After the sheet has dried, lay it on the floor. Divide the children into teams. Standing five to ten feet from the sheet, members of each team should toss a beanbag and try to land it on a shape. If the beanbag lands on a shape and the child can name that shape, that side scores a point. (Decide what score should determine the winner.)

WHAT TO TALK ABOUT:

Discuss shapes and the similarities and differences between them.

MATH MOBILES

WHAT YOU'RE TEACHING:

Color and shape identification, number identification

MATERIALS NEEDED:

Construction paper, yarn, scissors, glue, shape patterns, number patterns, coat hangers

WHAT YOU DO:

A great help for learning any concept is exposure to the concept on a long-term basis. This activity provides long-term exposure to shapes, colors, and numerals.

Pass out different colored shape patterns (circle, square, triangle, and rectangle) and patterns for numbers one through nine. Then pass out yarn and glue.

First, have the children cut out the shapes and numbers. Help them glue their shapes to the yarn and allow them to dry. After they dry, tie the pieces of yarn to coat hangers to make mobiles. The mobiles may be made from shapes, numbers, or a combination of both.

WHAT TO TALK ABOUT:

Discuss colors of shapes and numerals. Why doesn't the color change the shape? Talk about numbers and the relationship between colors and numbers.

SIMPLE MATHEMATICAL OPERATIONS USING MANIPULATIVES

- Grab, Guess, And Count.........120
- Counting The Pins..................121
- Counting And Recording.........122
- Necklace Or Bracelet 123
- Making A Counting Apparatus..124
- My Name Is Two 125
- Bean Race 126
- Using The Number Line 127
- Simple Sentence Problems - Subtraction...........128
- Mathematical Train 129
- Starting In The Middle............130
- Playing With Toothpicks 131

GRAB, GUESS, AND COUNT

WHAT YOU'RE TEACHING:

Simple addition and subtraction, estimation, counting

MATERIALS NEEDED:

A cloth bag; a large number of items that are fairly small such as jacks, erasers, marbles; small to medium-sized rocks; other items of a similar size

WHAT YOU DO:

Tell the children that you have a game called "Grab, Guess, and Count." Put all your items on a table so the children can see them, then put them into a cloth bag.

Let each child reach in with his left hand and grab a handful of items. Before looking, the child should estimate how many he has in his hand. Then let the child lay the items on the table and count them. The teacher or child will record the number.

Then let the same child repeat the activity with his right hand. The child will have two piles of items on the table. The teacher should instruct the child to place the items from the left pile in the middle of the table and ask him how many items are there. The child should count the items to see how close he was to his guess. Next, let the child see how many right-hand items he **adds** to the middle pile.

Now the teacher should ask the child how many items he got with **both** hands. To extend the activity, allow children to make a large collage using the items from the bag. Or they could write stories about what they did or draw pictures showing what has been done.

WHAT TO TALK ABOUT:

Guessing. Why estimation is important. Simple addition and subtraction.

COUNTING THE PINS

WHAT YOU'RE TEACHING:

Simple addition and subtraction, eye/hand coordination, learning math symbols

MATERIALS NEEDED:

Ten empty plastic two liter drink bottles, softball

WHAT YOU DO:

Discuss bowling with the children. Most have probably bowled or seen bowling on TV. Show the children the materials and tell them they will bowl in the classroom.

Mark off a lane with masking tape, and use spots of the tape to mark where the pins will be placed. Each child will get a chance to bowl. Before a child bowls, write the number ten on the board.

After the child has bowled, ask him to count the number of pins he knocked down. Write that number on the chalkboard under the number ten. Write the minus sign. Ask the child to count the number of pins left standing, and put that number on the board for the answer. Say, "You started with ten pins (point to the ten), you knocked down four (point to the four), and you left six pins standing (point to the six)."

```
Started with     10
Knocked down    -4
Pins left         6
```

To extend the activity, use addition.

WHAT TO TALK ABOUT:

How bowling can be a fun way to help learn simple addition and subtraction.

COUNTING AND RECORDING

WHAT YOU'RE TEACHING:

Counting, simple addition and subtraction, recording with numbers, learning mathematical symbols

MATERIALS NEEDED:

Individual 10" x 10" flannel boards, different colored felt, ditto sheets, pencils, scissors, various seasonal counter patterns, large plastic freezer bags, crayons

WHAT YOU DO:

Help the children cut "seasonal counters" from felt using patterns such as, pumpkins, turkeys, snowmen, Christmas trees, etc. (These can be stored in large freezer bags stapled to the individual flannel boards.) Pass out ditto sheets with simple addition and subtraction problems. Write the problems using seasonal counter pictures beside each numeral (see illustration).

Using the large flannel board, work through each problem with the children. Have them work each problem on their flannel boards and record their answers in pencil on the ditto sheet. Let them draw and color with crayons the correct number of the seasonal counters beside the answer.

WHAT TO TALK ABOUT:

Mathematical symbols, addition, subtraction, counting. Discuss the present season.
Sample activity for counting and recording:

```
    4   ****
  + 2   **      Could be pumpkins, turkeys, etc.
    6   ******
```

NECKLACE OR BRACELET

WHAT YOU'RE TEACHING:

Math vocabulary (more than, fewer, most, least), simple addition and subtraction, patterns

MATERIALS NEEDED:

Macaroni (10 pieces for each child and teacher), crayons, string

WHAT YOU DO:

Be sure you have enough macaroni for all the class and the teacher to have at least ten pieces. Divide the macaroni into three piles. Divide the children into three groups and have each group color its pile of macaroni with crayons. (Color one pile red, one pile green, and the other pile yellow.) After the macaroni is colored, divide among students, and make sure everyone has some of each color.
Let students thread an uncolored piece of macaroni on their string and tie a knot at the bottom to keep it from falling off.
You should make a pattern with your macaroni and let the children copy it. (Each time, let the children count how many pieces of the macaroni have been used and how many are left in each pile.)
After the children have reproduced several patterns, let them make a pattern of their own. Compare and find some who have less macaroni than others, some who have more than others, then some who have the same number as the others. Who has the most and who has the least macaroni on the string?
When all the activities have been completed, allow the children to design a necklace or bracelet to take home.

WHAT TO TALK ABOUT:

More than, fewer than, most, least; "taking away" means subtraction, "adding to" means addition.

MAKING A COUNTING APPARATUS

WHAT YOU'RE TEACHING:

Constructing a counter, simple addition and subtraction, introduction to linear math problems

MATERIALS NEEDED:

Styrofoam cups, string, toothpicks, wooden beads or buttons with a hole in center

WHAT YOU DO:

Demonstrate making a counter to the children, then help them make their own. Using half of a toothpick, punch a hole in the side of each cup at the same place. Thread one end of the string through the hole in one cup, and then reaching inside the cup, tie the string to the toothpick half.
This should anchor the string in the cup. String ten beads or buttons on the string from the end without the cup. Next, anchor the second end as you did the first.

WHAT TO TALK ABOUT:

What did people use to help solve math problems before they had calculators or adding machines? What kind of problems could be solved using a computer?

MY NAME IS TWO

WHAT YOU'RE TEACHING:

Number recognition, simple addition and subtraction

MATERIALS NEEDED:

Construction paper, yarn, felt-tip pens, hole punch

WHAT YOU DO:

Help each child trace a large circle from construction paper. Let each cut out his circles. Help the children put a number beginning with "one" on each circle. Punch a hole in the edge of the circle above the number and thread a piece of yarn through the hole. Tie the yarn using a long enough piece to provide each child with a number necklace.
The remainder of the day, address individual children by their numbers rather than their names. They should refer to each other by their number name rather than their real names. Using groups of children, do simple addition and subtraction by moving different groups of children. At this point, use each child as "one" without referring to the number.

WHAT TO TALK ABOUT:

Talk about simple addition, that is, adding one or two children to a group of children. Discuss simple subtraction – taking away one or two of the children from a group and counting the remainder.

BEAN RACE

WHAT YOU'RE TEACHING:

Simple addition and subtraction, using counters

MATERIALS NEEDED:

Three different colored groups of butterbean markers, chalk, stopwatch, chalkboard

WHAT YOU DO:

This activity should be used only after the children are familiar with using counters. Divide the children into three groups, and put them at three different tables. Give each group a pile of butterbean markers. Explain the rules of the game. Write on the chalkboard the numerals one through ten. Tell the children you will give each table a problem, one table at a time. Example: "Two beans plus two beans." The answers are on the board.
As soon as you state the problem, start the stopwatch. The children should solve the problem with their butterbean counters. One child should run up to the chalkboard and put a mark under the right answer on the board.
Then stop the stopwatch and write down the number of seconds it took that table to solve the problem. Do the same for the other two tables as they solve their problem. In all, you will give each table five problems, one at a time, record the seconds it took them to solve the problem, and at the end of the game add the total seconds for each table to see who was the fastest.

WHAT TO TALK ABOUT:

How to use counters. Definitions of such words as: plus, minus, add to, take away.

USING THE NUMBER LINE

WHAT YOU'RE TEACHING:

Number line, simple addition, mathematical symbols

MATERIALS NEEDED:

A commercial number line numbered 1-10 or one drawn on the chalkboard, pencils, paper, stuffed bear

WHAT YOU DO:

If the children have not been introduced to the number line, introduce them to this concept. Review the numbers one through ten.
Introduce the children to Barney Bear (the bear you brought to school). Put Barney on the first square, and tell them that this is where Barney lives. Tell them that Barney lives in a house on number 1 but wants to move to number 3. Ask if anyone knows how many blocks Barney will have to move. After the children answer the question, show them how they can find the correct answer. Have Barney move one space from where he lives and then one space (block) more so the children can see that he has to move two blocks.
Tell them Barney was on number 1, moved 2 blocks, and now is on number three. Show the children how to use the number line to solve the problem. To extend the activity, make a number line on the floor with masking tape. Write a problem on the board:

$$\begin{array}{r} 2 \\ +3 \\ \hline 5 \end{array}$$

Tell the children that to solve the problem, they should stand on the "3," (the bottom number) then hop the same number of times as the top number. The number they land on should be the answer.

WHAT TO TALK ABOUT:

About the number line, how "plus" means "add to"; problem-solving using simple addition.

SIMPLE SENTENCE PROBLEMS - SUBTRACTION

WHAT YOU'RE TEACHING:

Developing concepts about sentence problems, mathematical symbols, and simple subtraction.

MATERIALS NEEDED:

Comic strips from newspapers and comic books, construction paper, glue, scissors, chalk

WHAT YOU DO:

Write on the chalkboard the subtraction and equal signs. Discuss these signs pointing out that the minus sign means "to take away."

Pass out construction paper, scissors, glue, and comic strips. Each child should cut apart a comic strip, arrange it back into its proper sequence, and glue the pieces horizontally on the construction paper. Tell the children to add the subtraction sign on their strip.

Pass one or two picture strips to the children and have them glue the strips on the right side of the subtraction sign. Tell them to put the equal sign at the end. Tell the children, "We want to know how many we will have left."

Help the children make an "X" on one picture on the "take away" side and one on the other side. After the children have crossed out the one or two pictures on the right side and marked out the corresponding number on the left, the children should count the pictures without an "X" and put that number on the right side of the equal sign. (This activity can also be used for addition.)

WHAT TO TALK ABOUT:

Discuss the minus sign and what it means. Discuss the equal sign and why we use it. Discuss some problems written horizontally and vertically. Discuss that no matter how the problem is written, (horizontally or vertically), it is **solved** the same way.

MATHEMATICAL TRAIN

WHAT YOU'RE TEACHING:

Simple addition and subtraction, ordering numbers

MATERIALS NEEDED:

Construction paper, scissors, felt-tip markers, simple pattern for a train engine, simple pattern for cars on a train, large plastic bags

WHAT YOU DO:

The teacher should prepare in advance using a pattern or freehand, a train engine and ten cars for the train. Number the cars one through ten, and each car should have a number of dots to represent the numeral on the car.
Put the prepared train on the chalk ledge and tell the children you would like them to make a math train as well.
Tell them they can use patterns or draw freehand.

USING THE TRAINS:
Put the children into groups of five or six, and explain that when trains are in a train station a "train master" directs the trains. Children in each group should take turns being the train master. Give each train master a set of prepared cards with directions. The train master should read a card to his group, and the children should follow the directions. Let the children help correct one another. Some statements on the cards may be:
"Make a train from three to seven."
"Make a train from one to ten."
"Make a train from one to ten, take away three cars, then count how many are left."

WHAT TO TALK ABOUT:

Discuss how a train pulls train cars. What are trains for? Has anyone counted the train cars on a train? How many train cars could a train pull?

STARTING IN THE MIDDLE

WHAT YOU'RE TEACHING:

Simple addition, learning to count without starting at one

MATERIALS NEEDED:

Styrofoam cups, package of beans, index cards, felt-tip pens

WHAT YOU DO:

Tell the children that you will help them learn to count and add a new way. Line up seven cups. Put an index card under each cup with the number ten written on the card. While the children watch, drop two beans in the first cup. The children should count as you drop two beans. Then call on one child. Ask the child how many beans are in the cup. Ask him what the number card says. Tell the child that he needs to add the beans one at a time until he gets to ten, but since he already knows the cup has two beans in it, he can begin counting with three and continue until he reaches ten. Repeat the procedure with each cup, but drop a different number of beans in each cup each time. Use different children for each cup.

WHAT TO TALK ABOUT:

Counting, starting to count with a number that is more than one. Adding beans is one way to practice addition.

PLAYING WITH TOOTHPICKS

WHAT YOU'RE TEACHING:

Simple addition and subtraction; grouping and classification; becoming familiar with squares, triangles, and rectangles

MATERIALS NEEDED:

Boxes of multicolored toothpicks, glue, paper

WHAT YOU DO:

Divide the children into four groups, and empty a box of colored toothpicks on each group's table. Have the children sort the toothpicks into color groups. Check around the tables to make sure each child has at least thirteen toothpicks of the same color. Take up the rest of the toothpicks. Give problems that can be solved with toothpick counters such as "2 + 2," "3 take away 2," etc.
After practicing counting, adding, and subtracting, have the children use the toothpicks to make shapes. Draw on the board a triangle, a rectangle, and a square. Let the children make the shapes and glue them to paper.

WHAT TO TALK ABOUT:

Counting, plus or add to, minus or take away; triangle, rectangle, square

MISCELLANEOUS

- Eat And Create 134
- Where Is It? 135
- Representational Math 136
- Positional Simon Says 137
- A Part Of A Whole 138
- Flannel Board Positional 139
- Beans And Peas 140
- Building Fences 141

EAT AND CREATE

WHAT YOU'RE TEACHING:

Classification, patterns, counting, creative art

MATERIALS NEEDED:

Boxes of assorted multi-ingredient cereals, wax paper, construction paper, glue, large bowls, cards prepared with shape patterns on the cards

WHAT YOU DO:

You may use one kind of multi-ingredient cereal or mix others with it. At snack time, furnish each child a piece of waxed paper. Divide the children into groups, and supply a bowl of cereal for each group. Each child should remove a portion of the cereal to test and create the patterns he sees. Have the pattern cards on display to remind the children of patterns. (Move around the room observing and helping.)
Suggest that the children classify and count their ingredients before eating. Encourage children to estimate the number of different kinds of ingredients they have before them. To extend the activity, pass out sheets of construction paper and glue. Let the children make collages or pictures using the leftover cereal. Let the children write and/or draw something about this activity. (Some of these cereals are nutritious.)

WHAT TO TALK ABOUT:

Discuss patterns and where they are found; classification and sorting; counting; nutrition.

WHERE IS IT?

WHAT YOU'RE TEACHING:

Practice using positional words to give descriptions, follow directions

MATERIALS NEEDED:

A variety of small classroom furniture

WHAT YOU DO:

Choose one child to be the "finder." Have the "finder" close his eyes while another child hides an object from the class. The "finder" opens his eyes, and the children, one at a time, use positional words to direct him to the object. Example:
   First child says, "Climb over the chair."
   Second child says, "Crawl under the table by the door."
   Third child says, "Look beside the filing cabinet."
   Fourth child says, "Look under the corner of the rug."
   Fifth child says, "You will find it beside the teacher's desk."

WHAT TO TALK ABOUT:

How we must listen to follow directions. Positional words can help us locate objects. Positional words can tell us where to go.

REPRESENTATIONAL MATH

WHAT YOU'RE TEACHING:

Developing classification skills, higher-order thinking (representational), distinguishing between shapes

MATERIALS NEEDED:

One large sheet of blue and one white sheet construction paper, white and blue tongue depressors, blocks and other classroom objects that are square and rectangular

WHAT YOU DO:

Discuss with the children the differences between squares and rectangles. Explain that you need their help to categorize them; put square shapes on the blue piece of construction paper and rectangular objects on the white.
Give each child a blue and white tongue depressor. Tell the children when you hold up an item that if it is square they should hold up the blue stick, and if it is rectangular, they should hold up the white stick. Continue until all items have been classified.

WHAT TO TALK ABOUT:

Discuss the concept of blue representing squares and white representing rectangles. Could blue represent rectangles and white represent squares?

POSITIONAL SIMON SAYS

WHAT YOU'RE TEACHING:

Reinforcement of positional words, concepts about bodies in space, spatial-relations, critical listening

MATERIALS NEEDED:

Items such as chairs, tables, boxes, blocks, and other concrete items

WHAT YOU DO:

Teach the children to play "Simon Says." The person chosen to be "It" is the person who gives the commands. When "It" says, "Simon Says put your hand on your head," all the children should do so. If the caller leaves off the words "Simon Says," the children should not follow the command. "It" will give commands such as,
   "Simon Says sit on the table."
   "Simon Says put your food beside the block."
   "Put a pencil under your foot." (Children should not respond.)

Children love to play this game and to catch each other making mistakes. They learn the correct response to positional words while having fun.

WHAT TO TALK ABOUT:

Discuss positional words. Talk about following directions. Discuss following the rules of a game.

A PART OF A WHOLE

WHAT YOU'RE TEACHING:

Beginning concept of parts making up a whole, problem-solving

MATERIALS NEEDED:

A package of sugar cookies, an apple for each child, two plastic pint containers, a quart container, knife

WHAT YOU DO:

Tell the children you have brought in a special treat for them. Open the package of sugar cookies, and give one to every other child. Tell the children you have discovered you do not have enough cookies for everyone to have one. Ask them if they can think of something they could do so each child can have a cookie.

One of the children will probably suggest breaking the cookies in two and sharing (problem-solving). Agree that this would be the right thing to do, and let the children break their cookies in half and give one half to a child who did not get a cookie.

Give each child an apple. Go around the room and cut each apple into fourths. Cut an apple for yourself. Show the children how you can put the fourths together and have a whole apple again. (This should be timed for snack time so the children can eat their apples.)

Fill the quart container with water, and let the children watch you fill two pints from your quart. Then let them watch you fill the quart by pouring in the two pints.

Put the containers in a sand area and encourage the children to copy what you did and use sand instead of water.

WHAT TO TALK ABOUT:

Talk about how things are made of parts. Explain the cup is a whole and the handle is part of the whole.

FLANNEL BOARD POSITIONAL

WHAT YOU'RE TEACHING:

Reinforcement of positional words, spatial relationships

MATERIALS NEEDED:

A flannel board with a large variety of cutouts such as a house, tree, animals, flowers, sun, etc.; large cardboard box; large chart with positional words listed

WHAT YOU DO:

Discuss positional words with the children. Tell them they will take turns practicing the use of the words. Set up a flannel board and display the cutouts. Allow different children to go to the flannel board and follow the other children's commands. Example:
    Put the dog beside the tree.
    Put the tree in front of the house.
    Put the dog behind the tree.
    Put the sun over the house.
    Put the tree on top of the house.

To extend the activity, have the children find pictures of representations of the positional words. Help the children label their pictures and make them into a book after gluing them to construction paper. Children can draw pictures representing the positional words. Display all their work.

WHAT TO TALK ABOUT:

Discuss positional words. What do positional words tell you?

BEANS AND PEAS

WHAT YOU'RE TEACHING:

Classification, sorting, comparing, similarities and differences

MATERIALS NEEDED:

An assortment of dried peas and beans; styrofoam cups; soil; paper plates; plastic spoons; a can of kidney beans, great northern beans, blackeyed peas, and green peas

WHAT YOU DO:

Arrange the children in small groups, and give each group a large assortment of beans and peas. Write the name of each kind of bean and pea you have given the children. Give each group cups with the names of different kinds of beans and peas. The children will know the names of some of the beans and peas but may need some help with the ones they are unfamiliar with. Allow the children to compare the way the beans and peas look, their color, how they feel, etc. Encourage conversation about similarities and differences.

After the children have sorted all the beans, ask them if there would be another way of telling the difference between the peas and beans if they could not see them (taste).

Open a can of kidney beans, great northern beans, blackeyed peas, and green peas. Give each child a paper plate and a spoon. Put a small portion of both kinds of peas and beans on the plate. Let the children compare taste.

Finally, allow each child to choose two different kinds of peas or beans and plant them in soil in a styrofoam cup. Later the children can compare the plants.

WHAT TO TALK ABOUT:

Discuss the size, shape, and texture of each bean and the taste of the ones they tried.

BUILDING FENCES

WHAT YOU'RE TEACHING:

Matching numbers, number names, one-to-one correspondence

MATERIALS NEEDED:

Tongue depressors, construction paper, glue, felt-tip pens

WHAT YOU DO:

Using tongue depressors, help the children draw a fence on their construction paper by tracing. After the children have drawn a fence, ask them how many slats it took to build their fence.
Let the children write the corresponding number on each slat plus a corresponding number of dots on each slat.
Next, have the children write the names of the numerals under each slat.

WHAT TO TALK ABOUT:

Names of numbers, ordering numbers. Ask the children to count the slats or bars in a fence when they pass one.

BIBLIOGRAPHY

Ard, L. (Fall, 1986). "Dittos? But parents want dittos." *Texas Child Care Quarterly.*

Baratta-Lorton, M. (1972). *Work Jobs.* Menlo Park, CA: Addison-Wesley Publishing.

Baratta-Lorton, M. (1979). *Work Jobs II.* Menlo Park, CA: Addison-Wesley Publishing.

Baroody, A.J., Ginsburg, H.P. and Waxman, B. (1983). Children's use of mathematical structure. *Journal For Research in Mathematical Education.*

Brown, S.E. (1982). *One, two, buckle my shoe.* Mt. Rainier, Maryland: Gryphon House.

Croft, D. J. and Hess, R.D. (1985). *An activities handbook for young children.* Dallas: Houghton-Mifflin.

Fountes, I.C. and Hannigan, I.L. (Spring, 1989). Making sense of whole language. *Childhood Education.*

Freeley, M.C. and Perrin, J. (August-September, 1987). Teaching to both hemispheres. *Teaching K-8.*

Furth, H.G. and Wacha, H. (1974). *Thinking goes to school: Piaget's theory to Practice.* New York: Oxford University.

Goffin, S.G. and Tull, C.Q. (March, 1985) Problem solving. *Young Children.*

Henniger, M.L. (February, 1987). Learning mathematics and science through play. *Childhood Education.*

Kamii, C.K. with DeClark, G. (1985). *Young children reinvent arithmetic.* New York: Teacher's College Press.

Kamii, R. and Ginsburg, H.P. (1984). Cognition analysis of children's mathematical difficulties. *Cognition and Instruction.*

Sherman, L.G. (March, 1988). Making the math/science connection. *Instructor.*

Werner, L. (Summer, 1988). Guidelines for preschool math. *Texas Child Care Quarterly.*